Ancient Japan

A Captivating Guide to the Ancient History of Japan, Their Ancient Civilization, and Japanese Culture, Including Stories of the Samurai, Shōguns, and Zen Masters

Free Bonus from Captivating History (Available for a Limited time)

Hi History Lovers!

Now you have a chance to join our exclusive history list so you can get your first history ebook for free as well as discounts and a potential to get more history books for free! Simply visit the link below to join.

Captivatinghistory.com/ebook

Also, make sure to follow us on Facebook, Twitter and Youtube by searching for Captivating History.

Contents

Introduction

Japan, the country of the rising sun, is today known as one of the most prosperous and technologically advanced nations despite not having many natural resources. It is full of hardworking, ethical people that live with a mix of old-time traditions and new-age progressive lifestyles. It's the land of famed and virtuous samurai warriors, for whom loyalty is everything, and of legendary and adept ninja assassins, capable of bypassing any obstacle. No less famed is Japanese art, unique in its style and form, from short haiku songs to breathtaking watercolor paintings, both amazingly vivid and simplistic in form. It's the country of Buddhist Zen masters, who were wise and spiritual, symbols of moderation and morality. At the same time, it's the culture of geishas, who represented indulgence, entertainment, and corporeal desires. Today, it is one of the most liberal and democratic countries, yet it still has an emperor on the throne and a long tradition of shōguns, who were more or less military dictators. All in all, Japan seems to be a country of paradoxes and oppositions, of yin and yang.

Yet it doesn't seem to suffer from it; instead, it is thriving, growing, and developing, and it has been doing so for a long time. From those contradictions, a sense of unity and pride arose, guiding Japanese history and civilizational development through the ages, leaving an unquestionable mark on the world heritage and mankind. But this is only the surface of an astonishing culture that deserves a deeper look. This guide will lead you into that dive, showing how those characteristics synonymous with the Japanese civilization gradually appeared, formed, and transformed through time. Learning about Japan's history, its past failures and successes and how they shaped their nation, will also illuminate how this civilization developed, while at the same time presenting a full array of interesting stories, persons, and events. Hopefully, this guide will leave you wanting to learn more about Japan, to understand its people and culture better, as it is only a first step in the thousand-mile journey that is Japanese history.

Chapter 1 – Origins of Imperial Japan and Its People

In the beginning, there was chaos. Japanese mythology, like so many throughout human history, begins with this sentence. Over time that chaos divided into pure heaven and unwholesome earth, or rather, the never-ending ocean. As these two grew apart, seven pairs of gods and goddesses emerged from the reed that started to arise from the watery surface below the sky. Among them most important were Izanagi and Izanami, god and goddess of creation. From the floating bridge of heaven, they stabbed the never-ending ocean with a jewel-decorated spear. A drop of water that fell from the spear tip into the ocean coagulated into the first island, the first solid soil on earth. The two of them moved to the newly-created land and later decided to get married. From that union, Izanami gave birth to other islands, seas, rivers, plants, and trees. During that time, other gods were created as well. Izanagi himself gave life to Amaterasu, the sun goddess, and Tsukuyomi, the moon god. With the two of them, day and night were created. This is how the ancient Japanese imagined the creation of the Japanese archipelago, a series of about seven thousand islands that spreads from the Sea of Okhotsk northeast to the Philippine Sea south along the northeastern coast of the Asian continent.

Painting of Izanami (left) and Izanagi (right). Source: https://commons.wikimedia.org

Of course, most of these islands are small and almost insignificant, but four of them stand out as the major Japanese isles. Going from north to south those islands are Hokkaido, Honshu, Shikoku, and Kyushu. And despite looking rather small on the world maps, Japan has an area of about 378,000 km^2 (146,000 mi^2). To put in perspective, it is roughly the size of Germany or the US state of Montana. It is a considerable land mass that is separated from Korea and the rest of Asia by the Tsushima Strait which is at least 65 km (40 mi) wide at its narrowest. That means the influence from the Asian mainland was limited, although not nonexistent as it was previously thought. The fact that about half of the land of Japan is mountainous adds to its inaccessibility but also reflects the volcanic origins of the archipelago. Even the most famous natural landmark of Japan, Mt. Fuji, is a dormant volcano. And as the Japanese archipelago is situated on the edge of the Pacific volcanic ring, where the earth's tectonic plates collide, it presently has more than 100 active volcanoes and often suffers from terrible natural disasters like earthquakes, tsunamis, and, of course, volcanic eruptions.

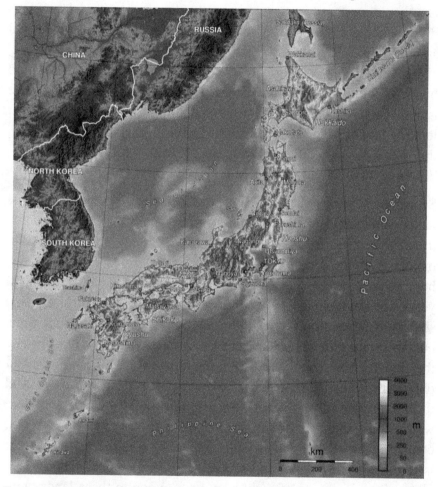

Topographical map of Japan. Source: https://commons.wikimedia.org

At first, it may seem that these islands aren't that hospitable because of this. Yet the volcanic ash created arable land, which constitutes about 11.5% of Japan's total area, making it rather fertile and capable of supporting a large population. The rest of the land is covered by forests, cities, roads, mountains, and lakes. Of course, the actual percentage of the land used for agriculture was way smaller in the past as it grew with the rise of population, which numbers today around 126 million. To put matters further in perspective, the entire population lives on about 5% of the land because of the landscape, explaining why most people feel this country is rather small. Another important characteristic of the Japanese archipelago is its diverse climate. On Hokkaido, in the north, winters are cold and summers are relatively mild. Honshu has a slightly warmer climate, characterized by a more distinctive difference in temperature between winter and summer. The Pacific coast of this Japanese island also has a somewhat warmer and rainier climate than the coast looking toward the Asian continent. Going farther south to Kyushu, the weather gets rather warm and humid with heavy rainfall, becoming distinctively subtropical.

Seeing how attractive the climate, safe, isolated areas, and fertile lands could seem to the early settlers, it would be easy to assume these were the reasons for the first migrations from the Asian mainland to the Japanese isles. But that's not the case. The first humans to settle there came somewhere between 500,000 and 30,000 years ago, though the general scientific agreement dates the first settlers to Japan around 200,000 years before our time. At that time, humans were still hunter-gatherers, so the most likely reason why they moved from mainland Asia to the Japanese archipelago was that they were following their prey, large game like deer and bison. And they were able to move there because during the last ice age there were land bridges, as sea levels were lower than today, that connected Japan with the Asian mainland both to the north, to what is today eastern Russia, and to the south, present-day China. This allowed small groups of early humans to move to these lands, with the highest estimates of the total population never exceeding 20,000 in that period. But around 15,000 years ago, the ice started to melt, as the ice age was coming to an end, and the land bridges were lost, isolating to a certain degree the remaining population on the islands.

At the same time, with a warmer climate the land became more fertile, and hunter-gatherer groups, that most likely never exceeded 150 people, started to shift to a more sedentary way of life, creating more specialized settlements that allowed for early primitive trade. Archeologists found evidence of obsidian, a volcanic glass used for toolmaking, being traded in an area that spanned over 150 km (93 mi). The trading zone of this material also crossed over the sea, indicating that watercraft were being used by a rather early era. And the earliest signs of pottery in Japan are dated to around 13,000 BCE, making them one of the oldest in the world, if not the oldest ever found. This is used to mark the transition from a Paleolithic to a Neolithic age in Japan and marks the beginning of the Jōmon period in Japanese history. It was named after a cord pattern, called jōmon in Japanese, which most of the pottery was decorated with. The first signs of a sedentary lifestyle have been found during this period, with the most important being the earliest indications of agriculture from around 4000 BCE, larger tribal villages with populations going up to about 500, and the pottery itself. But most of the groups remained hunter-gatherers with only semi-permanent camp-like settlements.

These groups were still largely focused on hunting and probably even more prominently on fishing, as it seems that the majority of Jōmon settlements were found on the coast. During this period, their societies achieved several important advances. For example, in technological terms, they developed the production of hemp clothing around 5000 BCE and lacquerware in 4000 BCE. In social terms, there are signs of spiritual development in the form of shamanism seen through ritual figurines, burial sites, and enigmatic stone circles. As uniquely specialized members of the community, shamans, along with tribal chiefs and perhaps the more capable hunters and farmers, were slowly starting to form an elite class, though it is still a matter of debate among scholars if the Jōmon society was more egalitarian or hierarchical in nature. However, it was by no means a completely isolated or homogenized society. It had various local subcultures and regional characteristics, while rice and millet were introduced from the Asian mainland, most likely China, around 1000 BCE, clearly showing that foreign influence existed. Before that, people most commonly cultivated the beefsteak herb and barnyard grass. The arrival of rice also marks the beginning of the end of the Jōmon period, according to some historians.

As the rice was brought by the newcomers from the mainland, the spread of its domestication is seen as evidence of the first wave of foreign invasion. It culminated around 400 BCE, leading most scholars to see this period of time as the definitive end of the Jōmon era and culture. The foreigners, known as the Yayoi, pushed the Jōmon people north. The Yayoi had narrower faces and were slightly taller compared to the Jōmon, whose males were on average 157 cm (5.15 ft) tall and whose females were only 148 cm (4.85 ft), both with a stocky constitution and wide, square faces. The Yayoi were also more technologically advanced as they had knowledge of metallurgy and were more focused on agriculture. For a long time, it was thought that the Jōmon people simply perished over time under the pressure of their conquerors, but recent studies by physical anthropologists confirm that their direct descendants are the Ainu minority that today live on Hokkaido. For centuries, the Ainu people suffered a great deal of oppression and marginalization by the Japanese people, who bear a much higher resemblance to the Yayoi invaders. Today, the Ainu are treated a bit better as in 2008 the Japanese government officially recognized them as the indigenous Japanese population. But the motivation and origins of the Yayoi people, as well as the actual scale and character of their migration or invasion, remains a matter of debate among modern historians.

What is certain is that by 400 BCE the Yayoi period began, which is named after a district in Tokyo where in the late 19th century a new type of reddish pottery was found, indicating a break from former Jōmon traditions. And it was a major break, as the newcomers lived in a completely sedentary agricultural lifestyle, based around rice cultivation. They brought with themselves the technology of paddies, making its farming more efficient. Thanks to that, rice became a staple food for the Japanese, practically one of their cultural foundations, which remains to this day. And with agricultural development came the population explosion. From about 100,000 inhabitants in the late Jōmon period, Japan became home to about 1.5 to 2 million people by the end of the Yayoi era in the 3rd century CE. With that came larger settlements, with the largest covering an area of about 200 acres, which was at least 3 times larger than any settlement from the previous age. At the same time, agricultural development brought about the narrowing of resources available to the entire community, and the first true elites started to appear around the families that had control over rice production.

A jar from the Yayoi period. Source: https://commons.wikimedia.org

This was further emphasized by the rise of trade between the tribes. Some were settled in the regions that had metal ores, which are rather scarce in Japan, while others had agricultural surpluses or produced silk (technology which was also imported from China), pottery, glass, or metal products. But the trade remained in the hands of the wealthiest, further elevating them from the commoners. With that, society changed as well. Tribes developed into more territorial chiefdoms, with warfare escalating between them in a fight to control vital territories. Warfare was the final element that solidified the position of the elites as they were the only ones capable of both wielding metal weapons and gathering large forces to wage wars. At the same time, prisoners were becoming slaves, creating the lowest social class, although it never became as influential as it was in ancient Rome or Greece. This social stratification was an important change, ending the previously more egalitarian community. And as warfare continued, chiefdoms started to ally with one another, growing through conquest and creating a large number of rather small political communities which we today identify as kingdoms. Their power also grew which became evident by the fact that by the late 1st century CE, they were capable of sending envoys to the Chinese empire, looking for an external ally in one of the strongest world powers of the time.

These connections with the already fully developed Chinese civilization leaves us with some rare detailed glimpses into Japanese history, as the Chinese historians of that era wrote about Japan as well. At first, they called it the land of Wa, meaning land of dwarfs, and they noted that it consisted of 100 small kingdoms. By the mid-3rd century, Chinese writers give us more detailed looks, describing in more detail Yamatai (Hsieh-ma-t'ai in Chinese) as the strongest of the Japanese kingdoms. They report this kingdom was ruled by Queen Himiko, a female shaman and a strong figure which was recognized by the Chinese as the ruler of the entirety of Japan, though it is unclear if her influence was that strong. She supposedly lived secluded in a fortress, served by 1,000 women and 1 man, guarded by 100 soldiers, and accessible only to her brother, who dealt with the day-to-day state affairs. Chinese reports tell us that Himiko herself was involved with magic and sorcery and that she remained unmarried. She ascended to the throne after a long period of wars in Japan around 180 CE, and she ruled until her death in 248 CE, which afterward Yamatai fell once again into turmoil. Reportedly, a king was chosen, but no one wanted to obey him, so a new queen, 13-year-old Iyo, who was Himiko's relative, was picked as a new ruler.

These details, like the exact location of Yamatai which some scholars place in northern Kyushu or central Honshu, are marked with a dose of uncertainty, as no other evidence of them have been found. No archeological sites have been unearthed, and no Japanese sources from that era exist, as later histories omit Himiko, either by lack of knowledge or because female rulers didn't fit the imperial narrative. But more important details are the Chinese depictions of customs and life in Japan, which historians usually accept as true. They note that Japanese people were fond of drinking and ate with their hands, which is corroborated by the lack of any eating utensils found in graves of the Yayoi period. The hierarchy was important, as people from the lower classes would step aside from the road and bow to the member of a higher class, showing his respect. Nobles were allowed to have several wives and usually had attendants or slaves. They practiced divination by burning bones, which was also corroborated by archeological findings, and buried their dead in a single coffin. The Yayoi Japanese made clothes out of silk, linen, cotton, and hemp, while they used bronze to make religious items, like mirrors or bells, and in some occasions weapons as well. Iron was usually reserved for weapons and in some cases agricultural tools, as it was more durable.

Modern illustration of Queen Himiko. Source: https://commons.wikimedia.org

All of those items, along with food, chiefly rice, was used for trade, which Chinese sources say happened in centralized markets which could be found in every district. And though modern scholars aren't certain how exactly those early kingdoms functioned, Chinese writers note that their governments were indeed able to gather taxes or tributes from their subjects. This meant that by the end of the Yayoi period these early Japanese states were growing into fully functional shamanistic monarchies with distinctive social stratification. The Yayoi rulers were indeed increasing their power, and their states were increasingly centralized and territorial. Those economic, political, social, and technological changes of this period were indeed a first step toward the unification into a singular Japanese state. And they also facilitated the creation of an amalgamated Japanese civilization, as in these centuries, there were many local cultural variations. As those transformations were peaking around the time of Himiko's death, the Yayoi period was coming to an end. The power of the state at the time became evident in burial traditions. Tradition states that her tomb was a large mound,

100 m (328 ft) in diameter, where her immolated servants, both male and female, were buried as well. Indeed, in the late 3rd century CE, burial mounds became a common tradition for rulers and members of the elite, marking a beginning of a new period of Japanese history.

Those burial mounds, known as kofun in Japanese, gave the name to the new era. It was an era where the power of the state grew rapidly, seen in its ability to create large tombs filled with various items for the afterlife as well as numerous weapons. Besides proving the wealth of the deceased, those arms were also showcasing the force that the elite was able to wield to protect its position in power. This rise in power was followed by smaller kingdoms or chiefdoms being incorporated or conquered by the larger and stronger ones. So instead of a hundred smaller states, there were several larger kingdoms. The most important of these was the Yamato kingdom, located in the Nara Basin in the southwestern parts of Honshu, between the present-day cities of Osaka and Kyoto. Because of the similar name, some historians link it with the Yamatai of Queen Himiko, but so far, this theory hasn't been proven. But the kingdom of Yamato did start to rise in prominence in the late 3rd century CE. It was a slow and gradual process as Yamato kings were expanding their power and authority primarily through negotiation, persuasion, and coercion and less through simple military conquest.

Later period kofun (upper image) and copper jewelry found in another kofun (lower image). Source: https://commons.wikimedia.org

This is evident by the fact that the most common method of expansion used by Yamato kings was to incorporate already existing states and chiefdoms into their kingdom, integrating subjugated rulers into the Yamato hierarchy by giving them titles and ranks. That way, they would become part of the ruling structure and less willing to rebel as they would have personal stakes and connections with the developing imperial system. Another benefit of that approach is that the kingdom of Yamato wasn't confronting possible threats around it; rather, they assimilated powerful enemies and then used their potential in further expansion instead of simply destroying it. A byproduct of that way of thinking and organization was the highly hierarchical social and state system, in which rank was the ultimate measure of one's worth. And it became such a staple of Japanese society that in a certain way it still lives in Japan today. But a negative side of that kind of expansion was that it was slow and meticulous. So, during the 4th and 5th centuries CE, Yamato didn't achieve absolute supremacy over surrounding kingdoms. It was, at most, the first among equals. But as no written records of these times exist, we have no exact details how this expansion and growth in power exactly unfolded.

What seems certain was that the Yamato state lacked a proper unity, thanks to its absorption of the other states around it. The main loyalty of a man was to his clan or kin, called uji in Japanese. One's fidelity to the Yamato king depended solely on how loyal the clan chief was. Those were more or less the outlines of the earliest Japanese states the Chinese wrote about in the 1st and 2nd centuries. The clan members became the militaristic noble class, creating a base for the Japanese elite that lasted until the late 19th century. The hierarchy was also strong in the kin organization, as all members had to follow orders of the clan head. Besides deciding the faith of the family on this earth, clan superiors were also tasked with appeasing the gods on behalf of all their kin. Below them were occupational groups known as be, which were social groupings of people related to the profession they worked in. This is why this class was sometimes translated as "guild" in English, but that is rather incorrect. A similarity exists as they provided specialized functions in a society, such as metalsmiths, weavers, priests, or palace guards, or even provided household duties in the elite's courts. But those were only a minority of be groups; most were in fact farmers. And unlike guilds, they had a similar hierarchical structure as clans, with a singular head of the family being in charge. And one's affiliation with a certain be was hereditary. Also, there was a fictional connection between the uji and be, with the latter being organized to serve and aid the uji. All of this combined makes be groups rather different than European guilds.

The expansion of Yamato in that period wasn't linked only with internal power and the rising of the ruling clan. From the 4th century onwards, they created strong ties with one of the Korean kingdoms, Baekje (Paekche in older transcriptions), which was located in the southern tip of the Korean Peninsula. As Baekje was threatened by the other two Korean kingdoms at the time, it started relying on military assistance of Yamato to preserve its independence. This escalated in the first half of the 5th century CE when Yamato invaded Silla, one of the other two Korean kingdoms, and for a short period, Baekje became dependent on Yamato. Baekje's crown prince was even sent to the Yamato court as a hostage to ensure this relation. It is in this period that Yamato reopened relations with China, sending ten diplomatic envoys to the court of the Liu Song dynasty by the end of the 5th century. It is likely that the Yamato kings did this on the advice of their Korean ally, as the Korean kingdoms had much closer ties with China than Japan in the previous centuries. These ties, especially the fact that the Yamato forces were involved to some degree in wars between Korean kingdoms, showcase how powerful this Japanese kingdom had become, evolving into a small regional power at the very least.

One of the reasons it became so powerful was due to trade, most notably with Baekje. But cultural ties were also created, allowing for Korean and Chinese influence on Yamato to grow, bringing various new technologies and knowledge. Most notable and important was writing, as it is during this period that the Japanese started to adopt and learn Chinese characters, which became the first script they used. At first, they were used to carve out symbols on swords, so the elite could demonstrate their supremacy. But literate immigrants became more and more appreciated by the nobles who saw the worth of the written word, slowly learning this important skill themselves. These contacts also refined rice cultivation and ironworking and brought horses to Japan. Because of this last fact, there were some theories that Yamato was actually conquered and ruled by one of the horse-riding peoples of the Asian plains, explaining its growth in power, but so far, no actual evidence for this has been found. Beside technologies, in the 5th century, the Yamato kingdom also started to accept two rather important ideologies from the Asian mainland. First was a centralized imperial government based on the Chinese model, which would improve the efficiency and power of the state. The other was Buddhism, which spread over East Asia from India. Both of these proved to be rather important for the future development of Japanese civilization.

But at the end of the 5th century, the power of Yamato started to fade as turmoil in its own territories started to erupt. It is possible that expensive expeditions in Korea, which did possibly result in some type of proto-colonial territorial gains, slowly weakened the central court as several other clans rose to prominence challenging the authority of Yamato kings. After several losses in Korea, resulting in the loss of all influence there by 540 CE and a failed rebellion in Kyushu in the 530s, it became clear that the kingdom of Yamato lost its previous power. It is at this time that its kings and court decided it was time to learn from the foreigners, to adapt their knowledge and ideas and strengthen their own position. With that, the Kofun period came to an end, but the foundation of imperial Japan was set and ready to blossom in the next several centuries.

Chapter 2 – Birth of Imperial Japan and Its Culture

As the old state system was showing its weaknesses, the Yamato kings realized the time for change was ripe. They looked at how foreigners, at this period the Chinese and Koreans, organized and headed their governments, and they started to implement a series of reforms that would essentially transform Yamato from a kingdom to an imperial state with an emperor on its throne. This centralization of state and culture is also evident in the name of this period, today called Asuka. It was named so in the 19th century after the new central region of the Yamato court, which was still in the Nara prefecture but several miles to the south of the old court center. That fact is a clear sign that the Yamato state was becoming increasingly centralized, and the first step toward this centralization was the expansion of the royal domain which began in the 530s CE.

This change was clearly influenced by the failed rebellion in Kyushu, as the Yamato kings realized that the power they accumulated from the royal lands situated around the court, which were directly controlled and owned by the royal family, wasn't sufficient anymore. To expand their strength and influence and regain their authority over their dependents and subjects, they had to enlarge their estate. So, the Yamato rulers started to create new estates, this time far away from the court in more remote regions that had important economic and strategic positions. These were managed by governors who directly answered to the king and whose positions weren't hereditary. This was important as it reaffirmed the reign of the Yamato rulers in lands that were farther away from their central region while at the same time creating new sources of income and military strength they needed to recuperate after the losses in Korea and the Kyushu rebellion. Further steps were also taken to increase the power of the royal clan. In the mid-6th century, around 560, Yamato rulers started to register and keep records of the households on their own estates. This practice facilitated easier tax collection and military drafts if needed, which further boosted the control of the Yamato kings. And later on, this policy was enforced throughout the entire Japanese territory.

The Yamato rulers didn't stop at increasing the level of control over only their domain. They also pursued the creation of districts, headed by district supervisors, which answered directly to the court. Districts were set up on lands that didn't belong to the royal family but to one of the subject clans in an attempt to create local governments that would strengthen the grip of the Yamato court over the lands that nominally wasn't theirs. Sometimes these supervisors were members or even heads of the local clans, but they were acting according to the commands of the central government. This was the basis of the bureaucratic regime that was created in the next century, increasing the need and importance of scribes. These changes in the administrative system were facilitated by the new wave of immigrants from Korea, which also provided the central government with the educated personnel it needed. It was a trade of a sort, as Baekje needed further military assistance, but Yamato was reluctant to help as it proved too costly in the past. To appease the Japanese kings, the Koreans sent their scholars and scribes to the Yamato court. In return, the Yamato kings sent them military supplies and, in some cases, armed forces as well but only if the circumstances were opportune.

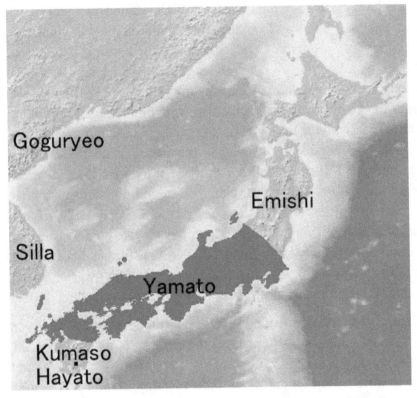

Map of the expansion of Yamato. Source: https://commons.wikimedia.org

The question of relations between Yamato and Baekje divided Japanese society, or at least the noble class. Some of the court ministers thought that sending more soldiers abroad was futile, while others saw benefit from those military expeditions. This led to a series of political clashes between some of the leading noble clans in 540. The result of these clashes was the rise to prominence of the Soga clan, which from this point onwards played an important role in early Japanese history. It was one of the first clans to achieve its major political breakthrough, not through war and martial success, but rather through methods of production and administration imported from Korea and China. And with guidance from the Soga clan head, the Yamato court adopted the policy of focusing government actions on accumulating both wealth and control, similar to the 19th-century Japanese motto "Rich country, strong army." As such, the actions in Korea weren't completely halted but were more carefully evaluated to maximize their gains. As this policy proved successful, the Soga clan's influence rose, with their head becoming the top minister in the court with the title of the great royal chieftain. The Soga clan even intermarried with the royal family several times, becoming Japan's leading gaiseki (in-law) clan. Their power grew so much that they practically ruled over Yamato, despite the royal family sitting on the throne. It was a precedent that would become a regular practice in Japanese history through the institution of the shōgunate.

Closer relations between Baekje and Japan, combined with the rise of the Soga clan, gave birth to one more important novelty, today rather synonymous with Japanese civilization. That is Buddhism, which arose in India around the 5th century BCE and traveled through China and Korea, where it arrived around the 3rd century CE, to Japan in the mid-6th century. According to traditional sources, the first missionaries were sent by the Baekje court as sort of a present to the Yamato king. It is disputable if this was the case or if the transfer of Buddhism started naturally with migration, but whatever was the case, Japanese opposed the new religion vigorously at first. But the Soga clan, who had adopted other Chinese ideas and technologies, supported it. And after several decades, when they became the ruling power in the state, Buddhism gained royal support from the prince regent Shōtoku, and his aunt, Empress Suiko, both born of Soga mothers. Buddhism for them was imperishably connected with the civilizational development and ideas that came from China and Korea, so the Soga supported this new religion as well. For them, it was a sign of cultural advancement. And with acceptance of Buddhism, ideas of Confucianism, Taoism, and general Chinese thought flowed into

Japan. It was the start of the so-called Asuka enlightenment, which bore a recognizable Buddhist characteristic at its core.

Prince Shōtoku played a crucial role in that, as he wrote the Seventeen-article constitution in 604 CE which heavily borrowed from the Confucian ideals of harmony and value in society. It wasn't a constitution in the modern sense of the word but more of a guideline for the behavior and morals of government officials. He also introduced a cap-ranking system in the Yamato court where the ranks of government officials would be differentiated by the color of their hats, a tradition found in the Chinese state system. In 600, Shōtoku and Suiko sent an envoy to the newly united Chinese empire, the first direct contact between the two countries after more than a century. This newly opened relationship only furthered Chinese cultural influence on Yamato. But reports of this Japanese envoy show another development in the Yamato court. Empress Suiko's representative introduced her to the Chinese emperor as the great queen (okimi), which was a traditional Yamato title that emphasized her relation to heaven, in a way imitating the Chinse imperial ideology that calls their emperor "the Son of Heaven." This signaled to the Chinese court that the Yamato rulers started to see themselves as equal to their emperors and they were angered by that, which soured further Sino-Japanese relations a bit. This shows that imperial ideology was starting to form in Japan, clearly influenced once again by Chinese traditions.

These political developments in Japan were further showed in 607 when a new envoy was sent to China. It seems that Suiko was referred to as tenshi, "the Child of Heaven." The parallel to the Chinese imperial ideology was apparent, but officially, it wasn't until the beginning of the late 7th or early 8th century that the Japanese rulers used their imperial title, tennō (heavenly emperor), for the first time. After they changed their title, official histories called all members of the Yamato dynasty emperors and empresses, even those who ruled in earlier centuries. In the earliest Japanese histories, they also promoted the connection of their dynasty with the gods. Emperors and empresses were descendants of the goddess Amaterasu, with the mythical first emperor, Jimmu, being her great-great-great-grandson. According to Yamato dynasty traditions, he ruled from 660 to 585 BCE, forming the state of Yamato itself. Modern historians have disregarded this as only legend, tracing the earliest possible historical ruler of Yamato to be the 15th emperor named Ōjin who traditionally ruled from 270 to 310 CE. And the tradition of calling the rulers of the Yamato dynasty tennō survived to modern times, and in most histories, those early kings and queens, like Suiko, are still referred to with imperial titles.

Prince Shōtoku and his two sons. Source: https://commons.wikimedia.org

With the diplomatic envoy of 607, Prince Shōtoku sent more than just the Yamato court representatives. He also sent a number of young men to be educated in Chinese schools and universities. This was another wise move done by him and Empress Suiko, as those men were going to head the second wave of reforms in the mid-7th century. But before they were to arrive back home, political upheaval shook the royal court. By the end of the 620s, both Suiko and Shōtoku had died, as well as the old Soga clan chief. As the Soga clan had heavily intermarried with the royal dynasty, the matter of succession became a matter in which the new head of the Soga clan interfered, trying to maximize his influence. He and other members of the Soga clan who held high court ranks started to abuse their power. This antagonized other nobles, even some distant branches of the Soga clan. As the years went by, new issues of regal succession arose, once again meddled with by the Soga chief. Finally, it was too much for the opposition, and a coup d'état was organized by Prince Naka no Ōe, the future emperor Tenji, and Fujiwara no Kamatari, founder of the Fujiwara clan. The Soga were accused of trying to grab the throne for themselves, and their most prominent leaders were killed.

After the coup, the new ruler of Yamato became Prince Naka's uncle, Emperor Kōtoku. Prince Naka no Ōe became the head of state affairs, similar to the position of Prince Shōtoku. Fujiwara no Kamatari became their chief advisor, with two more high-ranking nobles acting as government ministers. They also appointed the scholars that were sent by Prince Shōtoku to China, who had returned to Japan during the 640s, to serve in the government, as they possessed precious knowledge of the Chinese state system. With their help, Prince Naka and Fujiwara further transformed the Japanese administrative and legal system, continuing the Soga path of implementing Chinese ideas. These changes became known as the Taika (Great Change) Reforms, which unfolded over several decades and resulted in the final transformation of the old royal system into the new imperial system. The first action taken by Emperor Kōtoku and Prince Naka was to have all the ministers swear an oath to the ruler, asserting the principle that a sovereign and his advisers were to rule the state directly and not the prominent chieftains of powerful clans.

In the next few years, the central government under Prince Naka and Fujiwara continued to enact new measures aimed to increase the power and authority of the central government. They nationalized the lands, abolishing the clans' hereditary possession of lands, and then used the repossessed property to materially support government officials if needed. The government also took over the direct control of Buddhist temples from the clans, appointing their own priests. This was done to decrease the symbolic strength of the clans. With further reforms, they surveyed the lands and people to facilitate the collection of existing taxes as well as forming new ones. Most levies were now paid based on production, roughly 3% of the yield. But fixed taxes existed for houses and land, as well as weapons and horses. Furthermore, reformers seized weapons across the country, limiting rebellions by the discontent nobles. The entire country was divided into provinces, which were headed by government-appointed provincial inspectors. These provinces were further divided into districts with supervisors carrying out the imperial will. Below them were village heads, presiding over roughly fifty households and tasked with preventing and dealing with crime and enforcing the payment of taxes. Finally, imperial edicts proclaimed the allowed size of burial mounds for each class and rank, so even in death, one's place in the hierarchy could be known. All of the mentioned reforms undoubtedly show the direct imperial rule of the Yamato king over the state as well as the forming of the distinct hierarchical system.

Yet after several years, the spirit of reformation dwindled. The new system needed some time to work itself out and become fully functioning, and the reformists needed to replenish their energy. In 654, Emperor Kōtoku died and was succeeded by his sister. In that period, the Chinese empire, under the Tang dynasty, started to expand its influence in Korea and in 660 CE invaded the kingdom of Baekje, a traditional ally of the Yamato court. The Chinese were assisted by another Korean kingdom, Silla, and they managed to quickly crush the Baekje forces. Their leaders turned to Japan for help, but the Yamato expedition was delayed as the queen had died in the summer of 661. It was the right time for Prince Naka to take his rightful place on the throne as Emperor Tenji. He heard the pleas of his allies and in 663 sent his armies across the sea to help restore Baekje, but they were no match for the combined Tang-Silla military. After this failure, Baekje became a semi-independent kingdom under the Tang protectorate, and Japan lost all of its influence in Korea. In the next couple of years, China attacked the third Korean kingdom called Koguryŏ, which was located in the northern area of the peninsula. They also tried to gain military assistance from Tenji, but he realized that at the moment Korea was out of the reach for his state.

Despite their failure, this military and political defeat shook up the Yamato court, and the reformistic spirit was once again fired up. It was rekindled both by fear of a Tang invasion, which led to increased construction of defensive structures and forts, as well as the influx of educated Korean immigrants from the fallen Baekje government. Those refugees, as we might call them today, brought with them knowledge which was used to increase the control and authority of the central administration, increase its income, and strengthen the Yamato economy in general. Tenji's government recognized the worth of those Korean scholars and nobles and gave them lower court ranks to help further the reforms. The first step in the reform process was to once again reappraise and increase the number of government ranks. Then, in 668 CE, the first administrative law, known as Ōmi-ryō, was issued. This legal code was certainly based upon the traditions of the Chinese bureaucratic system and philosophies of Confucianism. The exact contents of the Ōmi-ryō are unknown as it was lost to time. This fact made its entire existence questionable to some historians, but through circumstantial evidence, it was confirmed as real. And though it was most likely compiled by Fujiwara no Kamatari, it was certainly heavily influenced by the Korean-educated immigrants. The end result of these reforms was the increased strength of the Yamato state in both internal and external affairs, driven by fear of a Chinese attack.

Later illustration of Emperor Tenji. Source: https://commons.wikimedia.org

Yet no matter how much authority the state managed to accumulate, it was still vulnerable to internal dynastic struggles. In 672, Tenji died, leaving his son and brother to compete for the throne. For a few months, the civil war disrupted the reforms. From the fight, Tenji's brother, Tenmu, emerged as the new ruler. Some modern historians believe that before his ultimate victory, Tenji's son managed to be crowned, counting him in the list of Japanese emperors. But this remains disputable and less important, considering that even if it was true, his reign wasn't longer than a couple of months. By the time Tenmu solidified his place on the throne, Silla directly challenged the Chinese empire and by 668 managed to unify Korea. This meant that the threat to Yamato wasn't coming from the Chinese anymore but from traditionally hostile Silla, which had now become a true international power. Looking at both Korean and Chinese state models, as well as

Yamato traditions, Tenmu set out to further strengthen his rule by building what was to become known as tennō-sei, the Japanese imperial government system.

To achieve that, as well as to secure his country from a possible invasion, he first reformed and unified the military. He created an imperial army, stationing it in the remote regions and around the capital, and then incorporated local clans into that system by awarding them titles and ranks. Thus, he made every local chieftain into a loyal military commander, increasing the strength of the imperial army. This innovation transformed Yamato into a clan-based military state. Tenmu then proceeded to increase the unity and loyalty of his subjects by increasing his priestly and spiritual authority. He started to emphasize the connection between the royal family and Amaterasu, setting the ceremonial and institutional base of Yamato monarchs as the high priests or priestesses of kami worship, a religion which is also known as Shinto. Furthermore, he finalized and widened the process of the imperial throne taking over control of Buddhist temples. This gave the Yamato state more of a theocratic character, influenced by the policies of Silla kings. Finally, Tenmu once again reformed administrative divisions of Yamato, its central government, and revised the Ōmi-ryō, adding new laws to it. Despite the fact the revision was done three years after his death in 689, his legislative reforms advanced Yamato toward Chinese-styled bureaucratic order.

Tenmu's reforms were polished and completed by his grandson Monmu who, after a brief regent rule of Tenmu's wife, ascended to the throne in 697. He issued the Taihō-ritsuryō in 701 which, besides adding criminal law (Ritsu), finished the institutionalization of the imperial government. On top was the monarch, whose will was expressed through decrees (mikotonori) and edicts (semmy). Below him were the Department of Worship (Jingi-kan), tasked with religious matters, and the Department of State (Daijō-kan), which was occupied with secular issues. The Department of State was headed by the chancellor, who was the ruler's closest advisor and most trusted official. He was helped by Ministers of the Left and Right and four Great Councillors. All of them together were tasked with making important policy decisions. Below them were three Minor Councillors, Controllers of the Left and Right, as well as eight ministries, which fulfilled and enacted the will of the monarch and the high officials. The entire country was divided into eight regions, one of them being the capital. Those regions were further divided into provinces, which usually had at least one military corps of about a thousand men stationed in them. Below them were districts and then townships and villages. Of course, the Taihō code also dealt with matters like establishing a 30-rank system of court officials, land ownership, registration of the population, etc.

With the Taihō-ritsuryō, the Japanese imperial system was finished, transforming the old Yamato kingdom into a Japanese empire. This can be symbolically represented with two examples, one of them being the actual change of the name from Yamato to Japan during the late 7th century CE. Chinese scribes up until that point usually called Yamato Wa or Woguo, which was belittling the Japanese by denoting their state as "dwarf country" and them as "submissive people," despite the Yamato court trying to use the same symbol with the meaning of "harmony." So, in that period, the royal court decided that new symbols would be used, which literally translated means "root/origin of the sun," or how Westerners today more usually say, "the land of the rising sun." When those characters were read, they sounded like Nippon or Nihon, which is how the Japanese to this day call their country. So, it was at the end of the 7th century that Japan was born from Yamato, which remained the name of the imperial dynasty. The second example was the birth of the title tennō. It was first recorded in the two earliest histories written by the Japanese, Kojiki (c. 711) and Nihon Shoki (720), and in them, all previous rulers of Japan are denoted as emperors, even the mythical ones that predated the Yamato court. As they were largely written to give credit to the reforms and rules of both Tenmu and Monmu, historians argue that it was one of them who first chose the title for himself instead of it being attributed to them posthumously.

Extent of Japanese expansion by the time of the Taihō-ritsuryō. Source: https://commons.wikimedia.org

With both of these facts, we can conclude that by 707 when Monmu died, the formation of the Japanese empire was both symbolically and factually finished without a doubt. It also roughly coincides with the end of the Asuka period, as Heijō-kyō (present-day city of Nara) became a new, proper capital, built with that sole purpose. But the state itself wasn't the only thing that went through a transformation and rebirth during that era. Influenced by Chinese and Korean civilizations, Confucianism, Taoism, and mostly Buddhism, Japanese culture and society changed and evolved as well. The social structure still relied upon strict hierarchy and clan division, which is still synonymous with the Japanese even today, but it was now more based on imperial ranking and administrative division. And art forms such as paintings and sculptures were heavily influenced by the Chinese style and Buddhist traditions, and they started to resemble the traditional Japanese style as we envision it today. Other art forms, like literary works, were for the first time created in this period, as writing itself was first introduced in Japan by China in this era. It is when classical Japanese poetry, also known as Waka, was born. But despite the heavy foreign influences, Japanese civilization managed to preserve its uniqueness, which it possesses even today.

So, by 710 and the beginning of the so-called Nara period, named after the new capital, the almost two centuries long birth of imperial Japan and its culture was finished. The foundations were laid for the Japanese state and society, which remained in place until the 20th century. And the base of its civilization, through cultural proliferation and growth, are visible even in the 21st century in modern Japan. Yet there were even more achievements to be attained by the Japanese in the following centuries, as this was just the beginning of their empire and dynasty.

Chapter 3 – History of Classical Japan

The imperial state system, which was put in place by the end of the Asuka period, was the institutional creation of the Japanese empire. The use of the tennō title and the new country name was its symbolic representation. But the Yamato rulers realized that they also needed a more physical representation of that crucial change. Once again, they looked to the west, to the Chinese, for inspiration, as they chose to erect the first real and lasting capital in the present-day city of Nara, in the region of the same name. Giving the name to the period that followed, this city was modeled upon the rectangular grid pattern of the Chinese capital Chang'an (modern-day Xi'an). With the move of the capital to Nara, which began in 708 and was finished by 710 CE, the imperial regime had gained a more permanent government, economic, and cultural center, as well as a symbolic and tangible representation of its authority.

Before Emperor Monmu died, he expressed his will to have his mother succeed him until his son became old enough to assume the imperial position. So, in 707, she became Empress Genmei.

Supporting her and acting as her highest advisor was Fujiwara no Fuhito, the son of Fujiwara no Kamatari, one of the leaders of the Taika Reforms. One of the first actions taken by the new empress was the aforementioned move of the capital, choosing Nara as the auspicious location as it was surrounded by mountains on three sides. She was also concerned about leaving her grandson a new and more imposing palace to rule from, which would represent their recently gained imperial authority. She wanted to support it with religious and spiritual signs of the monarchical grandeur, so Genmei ordered many new Buddhist temples to be built there, as well as moving and rebuilding older important temples. Thus, Nara became the holy center of the empire as well. Fuhito had his own reasons to support this change of capitals. First of all, the three mountains made this city safer and easier to defend. Secondly, it had a more direct connection via rivers to the Inland Sea harbor of Naniwa (present-day Osaka). This made its location economically more suitable and prosperous. Its rise as the political, economic, and spiritual center of a mighty empire became obvious as it quickly grew to 200,000 inhabitants, out of which between 7,000 and 10,000 were government officials, and covered an area of about 25 km^2 (9.65 mi^2).

But building such a city, with all of these astonishing building projects, took its toll on the state. It required a lot of funding and corvée labor, which is unpaid work done by the commoners for the state. The discovery of copper in the area near modern Tokyo and the subsequent mining of it proved to be an important boost for the Japanese economy, as metal was scarce in the archipelago. It increased production and decreased Japan's dependence on imports while at the same time facilitating local trade, as local copper was used to mint coins for the first time. But even that wasn't enough as surveys and reports show us that over 90% of the population was living in poverty or barely over it. In some regions, the percentages were even worse. It seems prosperity was limited to Nara and its surrounding districts, while any significant trade, production, or other economic aspects of life outside of the capital was almost at a standstill. Fuhito realized that this issue was rather important, and he tried to stimulate the economy by easing the transport of goods with post stations on the roads, lowering debt interests of the commoners, and preventing nobles from taking their lands. He also tried to make the local administrative system more efficient. Furthermore, the imperial government was spreading its control north, conquering new regions and people, while at the same time creating new arable land on its already existing territories.

Miniature model of the imperial palace in Heijō-kyō (Nara) Source: https://commons.wikimedia.org

However, none of these methods and attempts were enough to make life in 8th-century Japan significantly any better. Fuhito was aware of this so in 717 he started to work on revising the old Taihō legal code, adding new laws to it. But he died a few months before it was finished in 720, so Yōrō-ritsuryō, as it was named, wasn't enacted until 757. Despite that, historians today think that his work on this code did, in fact, manage to reinforce administrative bureaucracy, as it endeavored to increase state revenue and control.

It would be easy to blame imperial thirst for proving its might through huge projects as the sole reason for economic despair. But internal struggles among the nobles and the imperial family also contributed to it. Most clan aristocrats were more involved in intrigues, court affairs, and the gathering of influence than in actually leading the country. The political turmoil began from the death of Monmu, as not all members of the elite supported Empress Genmei, Fujiwara no Fuhito, and their pretend to the throne, Prince Obito. Yet thanks to the prestige and power of the entire Fujiwara clan and Fuhito's personal influence, they managed to stay in control. Empress Genmei and Fuhito even managed to make Obito, Fuhito's grandson, a crown prince in 714.

For unknown reasons, Genmei stepped down from the throne in 715; however, Obito didn't succeed her. In a unique precedent, her own daughter, Empress Genshō, inherited the title. In previous centuries, it was rather common for women to become crowned rulers but only as regents. They would inherit the throne from a male member of the royal family and leave it to the rightful heir when he came of age. For this reason, it is today considered that the rule of empresses was only temporary, despite them being fully-fledged monarchs with the same authority and obligations as males. This reasoning was later used to proclaim that male-only inheritance was a tradition of the Yamato dynasty. In fact, after Genshō, it became rather rare for empresses to ascend to the throne. At this point in time, only three more women sat on the Japanese throne. Nonetheless, Genshō's reign was secured by Fuhito, who was the strongest political figure in the empire until his death in 720. With him gone, the Fujiwara clan lost their controlling grip on the government as one of the imperial princes instead became the most influential figure in court.

However, that "interregnum" of the Fujiwara clan was brief, lasting less than ten years. By the end of the 720s, the government fell back under the control of the Fujiwara, or more specifically, four of Fuhito's sons. The regime of the four Fujiwara sons realized quickly that the economy of the empire was deteriorating. So, in the early 730s, they halved the taxes, abolished conscription, and founded charitable institutions and infirmaries. At the same time, Prince Obito, who became Emperor Shōmu in 724, began to express his

Buddhist zeal, building a wide network of temples, employing more priests, and erecting statues of Buddha across the country. It is likely he did this to increase the spiritual authority of the throne. Despite that, he retained the imperial association with ancestral shrines and kami ceremonies, which is linked with the Shinto religion. The Buddhist zeal was only strengthened when a smallpox epidemic ravaged Japan between 735 and 737, killing somewhere between 1/4 and 1/3 of the entire population. Among the victims of this disease were the four Fujiwara brothers, as well as many other high-ranking officials. The Japanese empire was devastated both socially and economically. This urged Shōmu to pour even more state funding into Buddhist temples to appease the gods. As the Fujiwara clan lost its representatives, Tachibana no Moroe, a removed member of the Yamato imperial clan, rose as the new leader of the court. He was backed by several smaller clans that were opposed to the Fujiwara, but friction between the Fujiwara and anti-Fujiwara camps continued.

It seems that Shōmu and his empress were also slightly leaning toward the Fujiwara, as they were the emperor's in-law family. Instability finally broke out in open combat as the son of one of the four Fujiwara brothers rebelled in 740. The central government, under Moroe's direction, sent troops and quickly quelled the uprising. Fearing further revolts, the emperor decided to move his capital several times before going back to Nara in 745. In those years, Moroe's regime tried to dampen the effects of the smallpox epidemic with several policies such as lowering the number of officials appointed in local governments and simplifying the administrative system. They also banned private lending and decreased the number of conscripted soldiers. But the biggest and most important change was when the government allowed for any newly cleared pieces of land to remain in possession of the cultivator. This, in essence, undermined one of the essential ideas of the ritsuryō system which stated that all the land belonged to the emperor. It did slightly help the state income, but in the long run, it enabled the accumulation of private lands and degraded imperial power. However, in 745, Shōmu fell ill and decided to make his daughter who was born by a Fujiwara mother his successor as all his sons had died prematurely. In 749, the old emperor finally abdicated in favor of Empress Kōken, marking the beginning of Moroe's fall, which was neither quick nor easy. He continued to occupy a high-ranking position in the government for several years, though his influence started to waver.

Emperor Shōmu. Source: https://commons.wikimedia.org

At the same time, Fujiwara no Nakamaro, the new leader of the Fujiwara clan, started to increase his power and position in court, and eventually, Moroe was forced to resign in 756. The rift between the two factions was further widened when retired Emperor Shōmu died that very same year, which led to turmoil in the court. Moroe died in 757, and as the opposition was losing its foothold, Nakamaro was given a ministerial position which wasn't constituted by the ritsuryō. The anti-Fujiwara faction felt threatened and tried to organize a coup, but their plans were discovered and thwarted by the Fujiwara clan. That very year Nakamaro also finally enacted the Yōrō-ritsuryō, compiled by his famous predecessor Fuhito. His ruthlessness in dealing with the opposition lost him popularity among the people. He tried to alleviate that by cutting taxes and military services, expanding the empire to the north, and colonizing border regions in Honshu. It seems that despite his unpopularity his rule was remarkably strong as no one could challenge him.

In 758, Empress Kōken abdicated in favor of her distant cousin, Emperor Junnin, who was nothing but a mere puppet on the throne. Though details of her resignation are unclear, it is not unlikely that Nakamaro had some hand in it considering that soon afterward Kōken started to oppose him more directly. A turning point was the death of her mother and Nakamaro's chief ally in court in 760. This rift between them was furthered in two years when Kōken became close, possibly even intimate, with an elderly Buddhist mystical priest named Dōkyō. The two of them started to gather Nakamaro's opposition around them, including some disgruntled members of the Fujiwara clan. It was enough to make him feel threatened as in 764 he attempted a coup. In a battle, Nakamaro's forces were defeated, and he was killed. Within a year, Emperor Junnin was exiled while Kōken was placed on the throne again as Empress Shōtoku. She then proceeded to favor Dōkyō, giving him ranks and positions, even considering leaving the throne to him as she was unmarried and childless. But the Fujiwara clan, who despite the fall of Nakamaro remained the most prominent one, didn't allow this to happen. So, after Shōtoku (Kōken) died in 770, they chose an obscure member of the imperial family, the grandson of Emperor Tenji, who lacked any considerable political ambition. He became known as Emperor Kōnin.

Under his rule, the Fujiwara clan continued to exert supreme control over the state. They cut down the number of administrative officials, shifted conscription more toward the rich, and became harsher toward criminals. In 781, Kōnin's son succeeded him as Emperor Kanmu. Early in his rule, he was a target of a failed coup led by other members of the imperial family, so he and his Fujiwara allies decided to move the capital from Nara in 784. The Fujiwara clan backed this decision because they felt it could control emperors easier in a new capital. Kanmu also sought to leave as Buddhist monks, thanks to the state-backed religion policy, grew too powerful and influential, endangering the throne itself as was seen in the case of Dōkyō. Thus, the Nara period had ended, paradoxical as it was. On the one hand, it was a time of great state projects, the building of an impressive city, and the spreading of culture in general. But on the other, it was a time of poverty and death, political turmoil and intrigues, without much splendor and dazzle. But on whatever side of the coin we decide to focus on, it was a period in which Japanese culture and history entered its classical era, marking how that civilization would develop in future centuries.

Emperor Kanmu chose Nagaoka-kyō, located 32 km (20 mi) northwest of Nara, in an area which was suitably located for land and water communication, even better than Nara. But it was surrounded by marshes and prone to flooding. In 785, the emperor's chief advisor and ally from the Fujiwara clan was assassinated in Nagaoka-kyō by clans that opposed the move and the Fujiwara in general. The leader of this opposition was the emperor's brother, Sawara, who felt endangered by Fujiwara influence. Sawara was exiled, but he presumably chose death instead. Soon famine, devastating floods, and widespread disease hit the city. Kanmu realized he had to move his capital once again, so he chose Heian-kyō (modern-day Kyoto) in 794. Thus, the Heian period began, marking the pinnacle of Japanese classical civilization. The beginning of this era was somewhat an exception in Japanese history. Most emperors before and after Kanmu were largely dependent on great clans, like the Fujiwara, being more in charge of spiritual affairs and acting as a symbol of Japanese unity. But Kanmu was different, and in that aspect, he might have been the greatest emperor in pre-modern Japanese history.

Miniature model of Heian-kyō (modern-day Kyoto). Source: https://commons.wikimedia.org

Kanmu became an emperor as an adult who was well educated and an experienced court official. Raised with Confucian tradition in mind, he lacked the Buddhist zeal of his predecessors and wasn't keen on spending state money on building extravagant temples. Instead, he was a rather pragmatic monarch. Circumstances around the time of his reign also helped his independent rule. Lesser clans filled several roles in the Department of State after the government crisis in the 770s, and with the last great Fujiwara leader assassinated in 785, Kanmu personally saw that no new chiefs from powerful clans would fill any important government office. Instead, he put his own relatives from the imperial house in those positions or left them vacant. He also allied with smaller clans to counter any opposition from the major ones. Kanmu was also aided by the two moves of the capital as it was expensive for clans to move so often, which made it harder for them to focus on gaining positions in court. In the end, though not an absolute sovereign, his word was indeed final in the empire, giving him power that few emperors in Japan held.

Emperor Kanmu. Source: https://commons.wikimedia.org

Some of his most notable achievements were the further conquests and colonization in the northeastern parts of Honshu against the Emishi people. They were rather primitive chiefdoms; some of them were in agricultural societies, and others were hunter-gatherer groups. Their exact origins are unknown, though some have suggested they may have been linked with the Ainu people who currently live in Hokkaido, although no clear evidence for that has been found. The Japanese have described them as hairy barbarians of the north, and despite their savagery, they were respected as fierce warriors. Prior to the rule of Emperor Kanmu, some of their tribes were conquered, which led to an uprising in the late 770s, for which Kanmu planned retribution in 781. And despite all of the advantages of the Japanese empire, the first three campaigns against the Emishi ended either as defeats or at best inconclusively. For over two decades, the northern borders of Japan were under constant threat of Emishi attacks until 802 when the imperial army managed to inflict a major defeat to the barbarians. This victory extended and consolidated Japanese rule in the northern part of Honshu. The 38-year-long Emishi war was concluded inconclusively in 811, five years after Kanmu's death, with a limited victory of another Japanese expedition.

Yet this war and victory, no matter how limited it was, became more important for Japanese society than mere territorial expansion. Constant wars waged mostly by eastern Honshu provinces caused the creation of private warrior forces. They became the forerunners of the future warrior class that is so synonymous with the Japanese culture. Adding to that was relocating groups of Emishi people to the south as part of the colonizing tactics. Though many of those communities quickly perished, some managed to assimilate. Those that managed to survive brought their warlike skills to the Japanese culture, becoming possible ancestors of warrior families throughout Japan. But this long and tough campaign was rather expansive, and together with the cost of building a new capital, it put a huge strain on state finances. That is why in 805 Kanmu halted further constructions in Heian as well as further campaigns against the Emishi. He tried to relieve the pressure on his treasury by eliminating unneeded administrative offices, tightening the control of the local provincial governments, and adjusting taxes. Kanmu even cut down expenses for the upkeep of members of the dynasty by excluding imperial descendants in the fifth generation and after from the royal clan.

Fiscal responsibility was also a characteristic of his eldest son and successor Emperor Heizei who ascended to the throne in 806. This made him rather unpopular among the nobility, who also disliked his scandal-prone behavior. But in 810, he became gravely ill, so he abdicated in favor of his younger brother Emperor Saga. However, soon after his retirement, Heizei moved to Nara and with the help of one part of the Fujiwara clan tried to rebel against Saga. Their plans were thwarted, and Heizei was sent to a Buddhist monastery while the rebellious Fujiwara were exiled. Saga himself became the pillar of imperial rule, as he inherited his father's erudition and his skill in administration. He abdicated in favor of his brother Emperor Junna in 823 but remained a vital force behind the dynastic authority as he retained a lot of power and influence. Until his death in 842, Fujiwara influence in the court was limited, which meant the Japanese monarch managed to retain their authority. Their limited influence at court was partially intentional as Saga was careful not to create strong martial connections with them and to avoid giving too many Fujiwara high-ranking offices. He also created a clan consisting of former imperial family members named Minamoto (sometimes called Genji) which also served as a counterweight to the Fujiwara clan. But the Fujiwara helped as well in this loss of power as they themselves broke off into several houses which fought amongst themselves for power, decreasing their influence in the court.

Emperor Saga. Source: https://commons.wikimedia.org

Saga's influence was powerful enough to guide the imperial house through another abdication, as in 833 Junna gave up the throne in favor of Emperor Ninmyō. As Saga's son, he obeyed his father by promoting Junna's son as his crown prince and successor. During the first half of the 9th century, despite all the efforts of Saga and Junna to adapt the ritsuryō system to newly developing social and economic circumstances, the central government was slowly losing its control. This trend was helped by the fact that the nobles and imperial family members were slowly starting to accumulate private land through grants or cultivation of new parcels. So, when Saga died in 842, the Yamato dynasty lost their much-needed and capable leader who managed to preserve imperial rule. Within weeks, the royal court was split into two factions. The crown prince, Junna's son, felt that his position was in danger. Both Junna and Saga were dead, so he, rightfully it seems, presumed that Ninmyō was about to place his own son as his successor instead of him. So, backed by several important nobles, including some of the imperial line and Fujiwara clan, he plotted a coup. The emperor caught wind of his intentions and acted preemptively. The crown prince was deposed and replaced by Ninmyō's son, the future Emperor Montoku, while several leading nobles were demoted or exiled.

This event marked a return of Fujiwara influence on the court as the new crown prince was born by a Fujiwara mother and was a nephew of Fujiwara no Yoshifusa, a powerful noble who was on the rise at the time. Ninmyō passed away in 850 and was succeeded by Emperor Montoku, who was now heavily influenced by Yoshifusa and his Northern House branch of Fujiwara. Yoshifusa took the opportunity to marry his daughter to the new monarch, and she became the mother of the future Emperor Seiwa. Yoshifusa also promoted his kinsmen to government offices, and ultimately in 857, he himself became the Chancellor (Daijō-daiji), the highest office in the government. Within a year, Montoku died, and Yoshifusa's grandson became the new emperor. Through this, his position was further solidified as he became Seiwa's regent, a position which was officially recognized in 866 when he was awarded the title of sesshō (regent). As the years went by, Yoshifusa purged the court of his political opponents, and by the time of his death in 872, his prestige and sway over state affairs were greater than any noble in the past. In essence, he became an emperor without a crown or a throne.

But as he couldn't have his own son, Yoshifusa adopted his brother's son, which was a common practice at the time. His adopted heir, Fujiwara no Mototsune, continued in his footsteps. He became the regent of seven-year-old Emperor Yōzei in 876 when Seiwa abdicated. Yōzei grew to be a rather violent person, with many comparing him to the famously cruel Roman Emperor Caligula, with some stories implicating him in murders of some courtiers. So, in 884, Mototsune forced him to abdicate, choosing the elderly

Emperor Kōkō as his successor. This was an exception in the Fujiwara policy of choosing underage emperors as they were easier to control, making it easier for that clan to retain its grip over the court. It is possible that he was chosen to restore some of the imperial prestige lost with Yōzei's viciousness. Kōkō's son Uda inherited the throne in 887 after his father died. During the next year, Mototsune was awarded the newly created title of kampaku ("internuncio"), with which he and all later holders of the title became the regents of the adult emperors. The Yamato dynasty could do little about this but watch as they lost their control over the country. This precedent meant the Fujiwara regency was fully established, making them more important and influential than the emperors themselves, as imperial authority declined and their position became merely symbolic. It is worth noting that it is mostly because of this that the practice from the Nara and Asuka periods of sisters and mothers acting as regents was lost. That tradition was used to prevent the dissolution of imperial authority from the Yamato dynasty, but the Fujiwara clearly had no use for that practice as they themselves were the ones who usurped the power.

Unfortunately for the Fujiwara clan, in 891 Mototsune died without leaving a competent heir. That gave Uda some room to restore imperial power, opting to rely on the nobility of a middle rank which had fewer ties with the Fujiwara. One of them was Sugawara no Michizane, a provincial governor who was a scholar-official, a bureaucrat specially educated for administrative positions who had in-depth understandings of issues that troubled the government. He rose to become Minister of the Right, which was unprecedented for a noble of his rank. But as a pragmatic bureaucrat, he advocated for reworking the statutory code, adjusting it to the new circumstances in local administration. Michizane realized from his own experiences that governors were unable to fulfill their tasks properly as the ritsuryō system was falling apart with the rise of provincial gentry with large properties, growth of the vagrant population, and the distortion of population registers. Despite the soundness of his proposals, Michizane's ideas were rejected. His position was weakened when Uda abdicated in favor of his son, Daigo, who became the new emperor in 897. By that time, Fujiwara no Tokihira, Mototsune's son, had matured enough to clash with Michizane in a scramble for power. Tokihira proved to be a better politician, managing to persuade young Daigo that Uda and Michizane had conspired against him. For that, Michizane was demoted and exiled. Yet Tokihira's victory was short as he himself died in 909, leaving once again the Fujiwara clan without a strong chief.

For the remainder of his rule, Daigo managed to reign without much interference of the Fujiwara, though their presence in the court was still substantial. Tadahira, the new Fujiwara leader, did manage to secure the position of crown prince to an emperor's son born by a Fujiwara mother, which was crucial for the return of Fujiwara influence. In 930, Emperor Daigo died, and he was succeeded by his 7-year-old son and Tadahira's nephew, Emperor Suzaku. Tadahira became his regent and in 941 took the title of kampaku when Suzaku became an adult. And until 949, when Tadahira died, the three highest offices were held by the Fujiwara—to be more precise, Tadahira and his brothers or sons. The country was once again in the firm grip of the Fujiwara. During the 940s, the central government finally realized it had to adapt to the changing economic and social circumstances. The government instituted land taxes in place of per capita taxation. It also accepted private land ownership, though it tried to limit its expansion, and it recognized local governments as quasi-autonomous units. Provincial governors from that point had only contractual tax obligations, which meant that instead of fixed levies, their financial duties to the central government were changing every year depending on economic circumstances. This weakened the power of the central government, eroding what was left of the ritsuryō system. Thus, modern historians often call this new forming system the "Royal-Court State," distinguishing it from the older statutory regime.

Emperor Daigo. Source: https://commons.wikimedia.org

These changes weren't abrupt; they were merely formal recognitions of practices that took root over the years. Yet the decline of the central government's authority was obvious. In the late 930s, a large landowner and descendent of Emperor Kanmu rebelled and proclaimed himself as the new emperor in the eastern provinces. At the same time, piracy became a problem in the Inland Sea to the west. The central government managed to suppress these threats, but the eastern rebellion pointed toward future developments where local chiefs and their private warrior bands, created through family alliances and mutual local interests, would combat for their own goals. This was shaped into a full-blown samurai warrior society in the 11th and 12th centuries. In 946, Suzaku abdicated, being succeeded by his own brother, Emperor Murakami. From that point onwards, Fujiwara chiefs were the ones who not only held all real power, leaving emperors only as symbolic and religious leaders of the empire, but also were the ones who chose the line of succession. From 967, the office of regent became permanent, lasting for about 100 years and entrenching the Fujiwara clan as the actual rulers of Japan.

Within that century of Fujiwara regency, their authority was pretty much unrivaled as they enthroned and dethroned emperors at will. Political frictions and intrigues were mostly between the Fujiwara clan members. In the late 10th century, the government did try to stabilize the economy, steadying the supply of currency and prices while regulating the growth of private properties which were excluded from taxes. Yet these attempts were mostly in vain.

Contrary to governmental and imperial erosion, Japan's culture was flourishing. During the Heian period, Japan was slowly limiting its contact with China and Korea. Fewer and fewer envoys were being sent, and trade became their only connection. This was caused partially by the decline and fall of the Tang dynasty in China, which led to a decline in Chinese cultural influence in Japan, allowing for more indigenous artistic expression. This was seen in literature with examples in poetry as well as in new styles like novels and epics, which became rather popular in the court circles and among the higher nobles. Even the lyrics of the modern Japanese national anthem were written in this period. This "Japanization" is also evident in paintings where the Yamato style grew more popular. It is recognizable by the vivid colors and imagery of court life and religious stories of shrines and temples. But the most important cultural innovation was the development of kana, the original Japanese syllabic scripts, which are still being used today. It was easier to use and had much fewer symbols, though they were rooted in the Chinese script. Despite this innovation, literacy was still low, limited only to nobles and Buddhist clergy.

In contrast to the cultural advancements, the economy was further declining. Trade became limited as roads were largely guarded, and it regressed to the barter system as the government slowly stopped minting coins. On the other hand, the aristocratic elite continued to amass wealth through their private tax-exempt properties known as shōen. And as the number of shōen grew, the power of the central government fell. In the 1040s, the Fujiwara government tried to reform the economy, mostly to increase imperial income. Those reforms led to the state revenue becoming stabilized, but it recognized a large number of shōen estates, limiting the tax base even further. In turn, this gave local landowners and nobles a looser hand, eroding imperial authority even more. It seems that the Fujiwara clan, as well as other court nobles, were more preoccupied with their own affairs, intrigues, and struggles for influence rather than the welfare of the entire state. It should be noted, though, that the ministers were indeed working on everyday governmental issues, those were pushed aside when politics demanded it.

With that, by the mid-11th century, Japan was slowly entering the transition between the classical era, marked by a central government, real imperial authority, and a statutory system, and the medieval period. There, the emperors would become purely symbolic rulers in a country divided between clans, backed by the warrior samurai class, constantly locked in a fight for power and supremacy. But the cultural achievements of the classical era influenced future developments of Japanese civilization, often regarded by later generations as the Japanese golden age.

Chapter 4 – Early Medieval Japan

As the Fujiwara regency was coming to an end, Japan was on the brink of change. The rise of local landowners, backed by their armies, gave rise to a strong military class. As the struggle for power started to shift from court intrigues to open combat, the importance of this class was increasing. This was the birth of the samurai class, who dominated pretty much every aspect of life in Japan for centuries to come, giving the Japanese society a very recognizable form for which it is known today. Yet this transformation wasn't quick or straightforward. And before the emperors lost any trace of their real political authority, the royal clan tried for one last time to reinstate their control over their own empire.

Like many other historical events, this one was also largely shaped by chance. In 1068, Go-Sanjō became the 71st emperor of Japan. His ascension to the throne came at the point when Fujiwara might was on a sharp decline, losing its tight grip on the court. Despite their attempts, they weren't able to block Sanjō's enthronement, so for the first time since Emperor Uda, the Japanese monarch wasn't born by a Fujiwara mother. And more importantly, Sanjō was an adult, having served as crown prince for over 20 years, and he was determined to rule on his own. Being well educated in the Chinese style of ruling, which was based on a direct imperial rule, Go-Sanjō was determined to undermine the power of the highest-ranking nobles. He started to appoint middle-ranking nobles to higher governmental positions while at the same time turning toward the Minamoto imperial clan to replace Fujiwara in the Council of State. Emperor Go-Sanjō also tried to regulate shōen estates by creating the Records Office (kirokusho) which had to enforce his edicts that stipulated all estates created after 1045 or which had improper documentation should be declared illegal and confiscated, those lands later becoming private holdings of the imperial house. This, of course, was also aimed at decreasing the power of elite clans, chiefly the main house of Fujiwara. He also instated several economic reforms trying to standardize measurements, the quality of silk and hemp, and prices, all in an attempt to increase the income of the imperial treasury.

From all that, it would seem his reign would be long and prosperous, but that wasn't the case. He abdicated in 1073, after only five years of ruling. His eldest son became Emperor Shirakawa, while his younger son was named crown prince who was to succeed Shirakawa according to his father's wishes. Yet Sanjō died within months of his abdication, leaving his ambitious eldest son to rule as he wished. In many aspects, Emperor Shirakawa was just like his father, ruling directly, bypassing the Fujiwara and other high nobles' interference through his own authority, and by relying on the Minamoto clan and middle-ranked aristocrats. Fate pushed him to deviate from his father's plans as his half-brother died from a smallpox epidemic in 1085. Shirakawa then promoted his own son to that position, instead of his other half-brother, abdicating in 1087 to confirm his new succession line. He retired to a magnificent palace south of Heian and for a short period wasn't active in politics, though his personal authority prevented Fujiwara regents from dominating over his underage son, Emperor Horikawa, a kind, cautious, and devoted ruler. Despite these characteristics, he is remembered as more of a figurehead for his father, despite the fact that Shirakawa at that time was only passively present in the political life of the empire.

Emperor Shirakawa. Source: https://commons.wikimedia.org

But when Horikawa died in 1107 with a 4-year-old son as his successor, Shirakawa had no choice but to place himself in power again. Thus, he finalized the creation of the insei system of government, where the abdicated ex-emperor serves as the real sovereign behind the current emperor, preventing outside regency from eroding imperial authority. He achieved this through the in-no-chō, the private office of retired emperors. Though many historians link the creation of the insei system to Go-Sanjō, he died too early after his abdication to assert any pressure on Shirakawa. But he did lay the foundations on which Shirakawa himself erected the insei system. Creating this system allowed Shirakawa to prevent his half-brother and his descendants to jeopardize his own imperial line of succession through his grandson, Emperor Toba. Later on, in 1123, Shirakawa forced 20-year-old Toba to abdicate in favor of his son. Shirakawa probably did that to ensure his own control over the court, as Toba was growing up to be a rather capable ruler, more similar to him than to Horikawa. Emperor Sutoku succeeded him, and for the first six years of his rule, he was completely dominated by Shirakawa. But in 1129, Shirakawa finally died, leaving a power vacuum. Ex-emperor Toba filled it almost immediately, finally realizing his own desires for a direct rule and affirming the insei system.

Toba's policies were almost completely different from his grandfather. He made peace with the higher nobles, creating his personal retainers from some of them, and supported the idea of shōen as he gathered estates for himself. The only similarity between Shirakawa and Toba was their devotion to Buddhism and temple building. Toba had also gathered significant military strength as daily life in Japan became ever more dangerous. After the war, the central government waged against the once again rebelling Emishi in the 1050s onward, there were more and more local unrests and clan disputes. The weakened central government also proved to be a fertile ground for robbers and pirates. Ex-emperor Toba countered that problem by making Taira no Tadamori, the leading chief of a warrior band, his own retainer. By the mid-12th century, it became obvious that military clans, or branches dedicated to war, were becoming rather powerful and important as Tadamori was given treatment that a high noble would receive, despite being from a lesser class. But these noble warriors were still seen as retainers, as evident by their name samurai which means "one who serves." So, many other nobles looked at them with despise. But for the ex-emperor, they were a perfect ally to pacify his opponents.

By 1142, Toba decided to force his son Emperor Sutoku to abdicate in favor of his favorite and youngest son, Emperor Konoe, who at the time was only three years old. It was partially because he disliked Sutoku as the choice of Shirakawa, but there were also rumors that Sutoku was actually Shirakawa's son. Nevertheless, Konoe died in 1155 without producing an heir. Thus, Toba was forced to enthrone his middle son, Go-Shirakawa, despite thinking he wasn't fit to be a ruler. But before he could do anything else, he died in 1156. That left Go-Shirakawa under tremendous pressure from his brother Sutoku, which ended in a battle less than a month after Toba's death. Both brothers had backing from some members of the Fujiwara clan, giving them political influence, and parts of the Minamoto and Taira clans, giving them military power. The battle ended with Go-Shirakawa's victory and Sutoku's exile. He continued to rule for the next three years, trying to restore the symbolic importance of the throne by rebuilding the imperial palace, which had burned down in previous years, while also battling the issues of improperly gained shōen estates and illegal activities of the major Buddhist temples, such as pillaging and extortion, which plagued the commoners around them. In 1158, he abdicated in favor of his son while retaining his influence as an ex-emperor, continuing the path of the insei government set by his predecessors.

But his own son, Emperor Nijō, pushed back against his insei authority. He was fully aware that Toba wanted him to succeed; however, the old emperor thought it was unseemly to bypass Go-Shirakawa and enthrone his young son. Thus, Nijō did expect to be given autonomous control over the state when he arose on the throne. And he had significant support in his favor in the court. This animosity was increased by a Buddhist monk named Shinzei who worked closely with Go-Shirakawa to reach higher positions in the court, aiming to restore the idealized glorious past. This caused the so-called Heiji rebellion of the anti-insei forces in 1160, but it ended in their defeat. Despite that, Go-Shirakawa gained little by this as Shinzei also lost his life in the skirmish. And so, a struggle for power through political intrigue between father and son continued until 1165 when Nijō died, leaving his infant son to rule. Despite this victory, Go-Shirakawa wasn't as all-dominating as Toba or Shirakawa. His military ally from the Heiji rebellion, Taira no Kiyomori, gained a high office in the government after suppressing the revolt. Thus, he became an important political figure as well as a military leader and grew too influential, proving to be a challenge despite being more of a friend than a foe.

In 1168, Go-Shirakawa arranged the abdication of the infant emperor in favor of his own son, who became Emperor Takakura. This complicated the relationship between Go-Shirakawa and Kiyomori, as he became the emperor's father-in-law. Until 1175, the two mightiest men in Japan remained cordial, but it was evident their relationship was corroding. Yet despite the resentment that slowly grew in Go-Shirakawa, he had to continue to rely on Kiyomori to subdue the ruffians, some of them being the armed Buddhist monks that ravaged the lands. But the might of the Taira clan grew too much, as Kiyomori was not only in the position of the old Fujiwara regents, but he also held considerable military might. So, Go-Shirakawa tried to politically outmaneuver him several times, which provoked Kiyomori to stage a coup in 1179. Go-Shirakawa was confined to his house, a large number of government officials were replaced, and Takakura was forced to abdicate in favor of his son from a Taira mother, Emperor Antoku. Yet the harshness of Kiyomori's rule, as well as his low-class origins, left him with little support. In the eastern provinces, Minamoto no Yoritomo and his clan challenged the Taira, starting the Genpei War which was to bring the insei system to an end and push Japan into the medieval era.

Before moving on to the war itself and the further developments in Japanese history, we should take a step back to look at the foreign relations of the late Heian period. As it was noted before, Japan was somewhat isolated from the start of this era, having only sporadic trade with Korea and to a lesser extent China. However, as political circumstances changed in Korea, Japanese traders weren't allowed to acquire goods from there, and so many of them turned to piracy, raiding Korean ports and ships. But thanks to the improvements in navigation, direct trade with China became easier, so in the second half of the 11th century, more direct relations started to open up. This increase is also connected with the rise of the Chinese Song dynasty and the rebirth of Chinese power. These relations also grew above simple trade as the Chinese emperor asked for the official Japanese envoy. Many traditionalists among the Japanese nobility were offended as this meant at least theoretical submission to the Chinese emperor. However, Kiyomori gladly accepted as the Taira clan was rather interested in connections with China, mainly because of trade. The resurgence of trade was important for the Japanese economy, as besides many other goods, it brought copper coins back into circulation across the empire. As domestic coins were out of circulation since the 10th century, this was rather stimulating for domestic trade as well as facilitating trade.

However, the renewed contact with the Chinese civilization wasn't enough to derail the unique socio-cultural development in Japan. In the two centuries prior to the Genpei War, the rising importance of the professional warriors, contrary to the earlier peasant conscripts, was irreversible. And they were tied to the traditional Japanese clan social structure as they were loyal to their local noble landholders. It is also vital to note that at this period these warriors weren't yet the knightly sword-wielding samurais. They were called bushi ("martial servitor") or saburai (earlier pronunciation of samurai), which were courtly titles of military attendants. They were chiefly horse riders who used bows as their primary weapons, resorting to swords and daggers only when they ran out of arrows. Two clans, Minamoto and Taira, both descendants of the imperial dynasty, managed to become leading warrior clans through fighting against the Emishi in the northeast, pirates and bandits across the lands, and suppressing local unrests and revolts. They were slowly bridging the gap between the courtly aristocrats in the capital and the lowly warriors in the provinces. But as their military might rose, so did their political influence. Soon they found themselves competing for supremacy over the entire state in the Genpei War, which as far as military might goes was solely a showdown between the Taira and Minamoto clans.

Painting of a battle from the Genpei War. Source:
https://commons.wikimedia.org

The war began when Go-Shirakawa's other son, feeling skipped over as a successor too many times, asked Minamoto no Yoritomo for help against Taira no Kiyomori. Despite the fact that the prince himself died within a few weeks of the beginning of the rebellion, the Minamoto clan continued the fight. Yoritomo used this as a justification to promote his own goals which were to create a system that bypassed the capital, granting the lands to his followers and making the eastern provinces basically his own vassals. He chose the city of Kamakura as his center because of its historical ties to his family. In the early stages of the war, conflicts were confined to the eastern provinces where the power of Minamoto laid, and it seemed Taira had the upper hand after winning several battles. However, the natural death of Kiyomori in 1181 weakened the Taira positions, and until 1183, both sides were primarily preoccupied with securing their positions in their own lands, avoiding large confrontations with each other. Then, in 1183, Yoritomo's cousin, Minamoto no Yoshinaka, managed to conquer Heian, which by that period became known as Kyoto ("capital city"). Taira fled to the west, taking Emperor Antoku with him. At this time, Yoshinaka tried to challenge Yoritomo for the role of the Minamoto leader while at the same time fighting the Taira.

Minamoto no Yoritomo (upper image) and Taira no Kiyomori (lower image)
Source: https://commons.wikimedia.org

Yoritomo realized that attacking the capital would be futile if he didn't receive support. So, he contacted Go-Shirakawa who gave imperial sanction to his government, giving Yoritomo a lawful right to expand his fight across the entire empire as he was designated as its peacekeeper. That very same year, ex-emperor Go-Shirakawa ascended his grandson Go-Toba to the throne, negating Antoku's position with that move. By 1184, Yoshinaka was forced out of Kyoto and killed in a battle with Yoritomo's brother. Then, Minamoto forces, once again under the unquestioned leadership of Yoritomo, continued westward to deal with what remained of the Taira forces. But it wasn't an easy victory, as fighting continued for another year, culminating in the grand naval battle of Dan-no-ura, in the Shimonoseki Strait off the southern tip of Honshu. In that very battle, the Taira started with an upper hand despite being outnumbered, both because the tide was in their favor and because they were generally better sailors. Yet the tides changed when one of the Taira generals switched sides. Seeing that they were going to lose, many of the Taira started to commit suicide, with Kiyomori's widow taking her grandson, Emperor Antoku, with her to the depths of the sea. Within a month of that battle, the Genpei War ended with Yoritomo's victory.

The end result of the war was the end of the Heian period and the insei system. Some argue that it happened that very same year, as Yoritomo was granted the right to gather taxes. But more importantly, he gained permission from Go-Shirakawa to appoint military estate stewards (jitō) and military governors (shugo), who both basically became the main government officials in the provinces, giving the military class unprecedented political influence and power. And as his warriors were his retainers, it meant that Yoritomo became the de facto feudal overlord of Japan. Of course, this feudalization of Japan was a slow process as the majority of the land remained in the hands of its traditional owners for several more decades. Nonetheless, it marked a great turning point in Japanese society and history. Other historians argue that 1185 wasn't the final year of the insei, as Go-Shirakawa was still alive and blocking the final step in Yoritomo's plan. The two of them were locked in a political struggle for power which was only ended by the ex-emperor's death in 1192. That very same year, Yoritomo gained the old military title Sei-i Taishōgun ("Commander-in-Chief of the Expeditionary Force Against the Barbarians"), which was given to the leaders of expeditions against the Emishi. With this title, later abbreviated to the more familiar title of shōgun, Yoritomo became the most powerful man in Japan, starting the Kamakura period and Kamakura shōgunate (or Kamakura bakufu). Whatever exact year is chosen for the end of the insei and Heian period, it is clear that by the end of the 12th century, Japan entered its medieval era.

Until his death in 1199, Yoritomo was the unchallenged ruler and feudal dictator of Japan, especially after his victory over the Northern Fujiwara branch in 1189 and the expulsion of Go-Toba from the throne in 1198. But despite that, he never tried nor showed any intention of taking the imperial title for himself. The Yamato dynasty was still the religious epicenter of the country and the symbol of the empire. But thanks to the slow changes and precedents that date back from the Asuka period, by the time of the Kamakura shōgunate it became rather acceptable for the emperor to have pretty much no real authority, leaving state affairs to others. Nevertheless, Yoritomo's sons weren't as capable as he was. His father-in-law, Hōjō Tokimasa, who came from a branch of the Taira that sided with Minamoto in 1180, became the regent of his eldest son Yoriie. Yoritomo's son tried to push back against his regency, so Tokimasa stripped Yoriie of his shōgun title in 1203 and had him murdered within a year. His younger brother, Sanetomo, was more compliant, and so the Hōjō regency, through the title of shikken, became a permanent aspect of this early medieval period. And within a generation, the shōgun became a symbolic title without real authority, just like the emperor.

But the Hōjō regency wasn't unquestioned. In 1219, Sanetomo was assassinated, and the question of succession arose as he had no clear heir. This gave Hōjō Yoshitoki, Tokimasa's son, an excuse to strike harder against his opposition. But the more pressing matter for him was the question of the next shōgun. He wanted someone from the imperial family but was denied by Go-Toba, who was gathering support for himself in Kyoto as he was trying to capitalize on the unrest of the warriors beneath the ruling classes and the affairs that were shaking the political scene in Kamakura. Go-Toba refused, using his imperial right of choosing and appointing high-ranking officials in the government, which in essence is what a shōgun was. Instead, he chose an infant Fujiwara to be the next shōgun. But then he changed his mind, refusing to install a new shōgun altogether, probably thinking that the Hōjō and the entire Kamakura shogunate was weak enough for him to restore the imperial authority. By mid-1221, Go-Toba declared war on the Hōjō, but his army, filled with soldiers all over Japan, was an incoherent and unorganized group that stood practically no chance against the well-trained warriors from the eastern provinces which fought for the shōgunate. Go-Toba and his party were exiled, and all traces of imperial authority was destroyed, leaving control over the state in the hands of the Hōjō regents.

Emperor Go-Toba. Source: https://commons.wikimedia.org

The system that was created was of dual polities, one in Kamakura, which was headed by the Hōjō designated shōguns, first from the Fujiwara clan and then from imperial princes. The other was based in Kyoto around the imperial dynasty and the court. With the expansion of the shugo and jitō, the power of the bakufu was expanding, bolstered with the military force at its disposal. Hōjō regents also acquired legislative and judicial powers for the shōgunate, or to be more precise, for themselves. Yoshitoki's son Yasutoki became the new shikken in 1224 and further reorganized the bakufu. He created a board of councilors as a governmental organ of the shogunate and then went on to promulgate the Goseibai Shikimoku, the code of law for the bakufu in 1232 which stipulated how vassal relations of the shugo and jitō should function. Yet despite the fact that his regency is seen as the golden age of Hōjō supremacy, his position wasn't completely unquestionable. Although the emperor's position was more symbolic at this point, he still presided, at least nominally, over a Chinese-style administration that covered the civil population in provinces that were still officially under imperial control. And from these, he received taxes, which given the right circumstances were enough to seriously challenge the Kamakura shōgunate.

Yasutoki's life ended in 1242, once again putting the delicate political balance at risk. That year the bakufu forced a change of emperors, enthroning Go-Saga, a man who wasn't a favorite of the courtiers in Kyoto. Yasutoki's grandson Tsunetoki became the new shikken and tried to reaffirm his position in 1244 by forcing the current shōgun Fujiwara no Yoritsune to abdicate in favor of his underage son Yoritsugu. In 1246, Tsunetoki died, being succeeded by his brother Tokiyori. That very same year Emperor Go-Saga was elevated to the position of ex-emperor, and with his help, Kamakura pushed Kyoto to update its bureaucracy according to its own scheme. The quick succession in both capitals caused several political intrigues, but the Hōjō clan remained firmly in control. Tokiyori even went a step further to stabilize his own reign. In 1252, he instated an imperial prince, Munetaka, the son of Go-Saga, as a shōgun. Thus, he had puppets in both capitals, which were coincidentally father and son. This managed to prolong the stability of the Hōjō regime, but in 1263, Tokiyori died, and certain instabilities started to manifest themselves. Most notable was the quarrel inside the Hōjō clan itself, as certain branches tried to challenge the main line.

This led to some minor administrative changes in the bakufu, but it was the foreign threat of the Kublai Khan's Mongol empire which reached Korean shores that managed to put aside all political turbulence among the Japanese. In 1286, Kublai sent a letter to the "king of Japan" through his Korean vassals, the kingdom of Koryŏ which in previous centuries united the peninsula and had some connections with Japan. Through a letter, the Mongol ruler ominously demanded a tribute and recognition of his supremacy. It seems that his ultimate goal was gathering prestige for his dynasty, not actual conquest. But both Kamakura and Kyoto decided to ignore this request. The shōgunate started to prepare defenses, realizing that the Mongol threat was both real and serious. With a sword hanging over their heads, the Japanese found national unity, and all internal struggles for power were ceased for the moment. Yet Kublai Khan was persistent in trying to solve this diplomatically, sending several more envoys asking for simple tribute and recognition, all returning empty-handed. By 1271, the imperial court received a final ultimatum from the Khan and once again did not respond to the request. The bakufu ordered that defenses in Kyushu should be prepared, with all soldiers from that region returning to their estates and by pacifying all outlaws through military actions.

With the imminent threat of invasion, the main Hōjō branch eliminated all their opponents in the bakufu in 1272 as they wanted to have a secure situation in the homeland. Sources tell us that the atmosphere in Japan was full of worry and tension, yet the invasion didn't come until 1274 as Kublai Khan decided to finish conquering the southern Chinese territories first. The Mongols then sent 15,000 of their own soldiers accompanied by 8,000 Korean warriors in about 800 ships. When they arrived, the invaders had more success than the defenders. They were better equipped, had superior commanders, and were used to group movement and fighting. In contrast to that, Japanese warriors, having no major conflicts since 1221, lacked capable commanders and were used to one-on-one fights, even in major battles. Slowly, the Mongol troops progressed. But those victories were only minor ones, and the Mongols were unable to establish a good bridgehead to continue their invasion. At the same time, they were slowly running out of supplies as they were constantly returning to their ships, unable to gather provisions from the occupied land. So, after several weeks, the Mongol army withdrew, losing about 200 ships in a storm. Nonetheless, this Japanese victory didn't eliminate the foreign threat.

A painting of a battle between Japanese and Mongol armies. Source: https://commons.wikimedia.org

Hōjō Tokimune, who was shikken since 1268, realized that further strengthening of Japan's defenses was needed. He ordered that both military and civil leaders, i.e., owners of jitō and shōen, to contribute to building fortifications and walls on the coastline. He further conscripted all warriors, without regard to whom they were subjugated to. In 1275, Tokimune organized warriors in the Kyushu region into combined units of two to three provinces. Each unit would serve actively three months per year, while in the event of a crisis all of them would be mobilized. This became a heavy burden for the warriors of Kyushu, but the shikken also demanded that the nobles live frugally so that they wouldn't burden the population more than needed. Finally, he replaced military governors in strategically important provinces with trusted members of the Hōjō clan. So, in 1281 when Kublai Khan sent his second invasion, Japan was ready, or at least more prepared than the last time. But now Kublai was determined to conquer Japan, especially as the Japanese had executed all the envoys he sent since 1274. For this invasion, he amassed 2 armies carried by 2 fleets, one from Korea and the other from southern China. Together they had 4,400 ships and about 140,000 men, an army comparable in size with the Allied forces attacking Normandy during World War II.

Later painting of the "divine wind." Source: https://commons.wikimedia.org

However, the Mongol army, consisting of Chinese and Korean soldiers as well, who attacked from two sides lacked motivation and coordination between them. Their ships were also gathered and built hastily, many of them not suitable for an open ocean. And they were met by fortified shores and prepared Japanese defenders. So, the invaders weren't able to create a bridgehead, withdrawing after fierce resistance. Finally, the two Mongol fleets merged and planned the final attack. While some of the attacking forces were on the coast, a devastating typhoon destroyed the majority of the Mongol fleet, forcing their generals to retreat and leave the remaining troops to be slaughtered by the Japanese. According to the sources, between 70 and 90% of the invading army was destroyed. So, in the end, it was both preparation, determination, and pure luck that saved Japan from being conquered. Of course, the deeply religious Japanese of that era saw it as a godly intervention. To Shinto and Buddhist priests it was a "divine wind," or kamikaze in Japanese, that saved their country by a typhoon, claiming this was proof that their country was chosen by the gods. This idea remained implanted in the collective consciousness of the Japanese until the end of World War II, where it manifested through the suicide pilots who took the name of kamikaze, protecting their land from the air.

This national unity combined with the tightened rule of the Hōjō regency was achieved by the Mongol threat. But with the enemy defeated, this pressure was alleviated. With the death of Kublai Khan in 1294, Japan ceased to be in any danger. But the bakufu leaders didn't want to relax their control, asking warriors to remain alert without giving them proper compensation. Tension rose among them, blaming the Kamakura shōgunate for their misfortune. And as years passed, the Hōjō leaders became less competent to command and punish the insubordinate warriors who then turned to fight among themselves. Issues of outlaws and pirates also plagued the rising economy of medieval Japan. While that weakened the military positions of the Kamakura court, affairs in Kyoto destabilized its political power. There since the 1270s, bakufu leaders practiced switching the line of succession between two branches of the Yamato dynasty. This caused too much bad blood between them. Despite trying to debilitate the imperial power by this move, emperors of the late 13th and early 14th centuries started to show less compliance to the shōgunate. Some of them even reformed their courts and tax gatherings to improve their own position and resources. This culminated with the ascension of Emperor Go-Daigo to the throne in 1318.

He was a capable ruler who through a stroke of luck managed to rule without previous emperors meddling in his affairs, as most of them were either dead or out of the political life. In such a position, he started dreaming about restoring the imperial authority from the "golden age" of Emperor Daigo, his namesake, from the early Heian period. Attempting to exploit the weaknesses of the bakufu, which were becoming more and more evident, in 1324 he planned his first rebellion, but the anti-bakufu movement was discovered, and Go-Daigo barely managed to talk his way out of banishment. He laid low for some time before arranging another conspiracy to throw over the shōgunate in 1331. The movement was once again discovered, but this time after losing his generals, Go-Daigo stepped forward as the leader of the anti-bakufu forces. This widened the support for the movement, but the bakufu forces won, and he was removed from the throne and exiled. However, this didn't eradicate all of the anti-shōgunate elements. Gathered around his son, the anti-bakufu, now filled with outlaws and warriors without feudal lords, started to cause trouble around Kyoto. This was when the Hōjō made their biggest and probably fatal mistake. In 1333, they sent Ashikaga Takauji to deal with the ensuing unrest, but he harbored antipathy toward the Hōjō and kept in touch with the exiled Go-Daigo.

Takauji, who belonged to a branch of the Minamoto clan, realized that his forces combined with the army behind the rebel forces were enough to topple the current regime. Thanks to his contempt of the Hōjō clan, he easily switched sides. Go-Daigo came back from exile, and together they marched on Kamakura. Sensing the imminent fall, another member of the Minamoto clan, Nitta Yoshisada, rebelled in the east, attacking the bakufu capital and destroying the forces of the shōgunate. The majority of the Hōjō that survived the fighting committed suicide. Go-Daigo seized the throne from the bakufu-installed Emperor Kōgon, and thus, the first Japanese shōgunate fell. With the fall of Kamakura, the early medieval period of Japanese history ended, leaving a formed feudal system and ideals to shape its future development.

Chapter 5 – Late Medieval Japan

In the early medieval period of Japanese history, feudalism and a militaristic society were developed, transforming the Land of the Rising Sun into the civilization we know today. It was a unified country with an emperor as a purely symbolic religious ruler, and it was divided between martial aristocratic clans which fought amongst themselves for supremacy and the title of shōgun. It was also a deeply religious country with an intermixing of two faiths. One was Buddhism which branched out into several different teachings and cults, and the other was Shintoism, the original Japanese religion which celebrated the imperial dynasty as well as millions of gods. But during this period, there was still a resonance of the classical Japanese society there as well. For one, the emperor still had an echo of the imperial political authority that emperors in the past held, while the supposedly all-mighty shōgun was overpowered by his regents like the old emperors were. Those remnants of the bygone era were to be lost in the late medieval period.

But before that final transformation was to happen, there was a rather short period in which Emperor Go-Daigo tried to revive the past. In what is today called the Kenmu Restoration, he tried to recreate the old statutory system in which civil nobles held all important governmental positions, answering only to the emperor, while soldiers were nothing more than just servants. He started rearranging his government, confiscating jitō estates and giving them as shōen to his noble followers. With this reckless dealing with land issues, he neglected to take care of the commoners, thus alienating them as well. But most importantly, Go-Daigo ignored Ashikaga Takauji's wish for the shōgun title. Instead, he gave it to his son in an attempt to control both Kyoto and Kamakura. This was the final straw for Takauji, and the former allies clashed. The emperor sent Nitta Yoshisada to fight against him, but he lost, as Takauji had more followers from the warrior class since they saw him fighting for their cause. By 1336, Go-Daigo was routed from Kyoto, ending his restoration and enthroning Kōmyō as the new emperor. In turn, he gave the shōgun title to Takauji, which marked a beginning of the Ashikaga shōgunate (Ashikaga bakufu) or, as it was also known, the Muromachi shogunate, named after a district in Kyoto where later shōguns based their headquarters.

Despite that, the enemies of the new bakufu weren't stepping down. Go-Daigo retreated to the mountains of Yoshino in the Nara Province, south of Kyoto. There, in early 1337, he set up the Southern Court that opposed the Northern Court which was under the patronage of the bakufu and still resided in Kyoto. For the first and only time, the imperial dynasty split into two branches that claimed to reign at the same time. Japan entered an era of never-ending civil war, as fighting between the two sides continued. For most of this fighting, the Ashikaga shōgunate had the upper hand, but for a brief period in the early 1350s, the Southern Court managed to turn the tides. Because of internal division, Ashikaga Tadayoshi, Takauji's brother switched sides and managed to take both Kamakura, which was still the capital of the bakufu, and Kyoto. Yet Takauji managed to beat him twice, restoring the supremacy of the Northern Court. He and his brother reconciled, but Ashikaga died rather quickly after this, presumably poisoned by Takauji. Left without a serious army and a capable general, the Southern Court returned to guerilla warfare and small skirmishes through which they continued the civil war.

Ashikaga period samurais. Source: https://commons.wikimedia.org

The long reign of Ashikaga Takauji ended in 1358 when he died, leaving the title of shōgun to his grandson Yoshiakira. Losing such a capable leader was a huge setback for the Ashikaga bakufu, and the Southern Court forces once again posed a more serious threat. But the shōgunate was strong enough to endure, and in 1368, he was succeeded by his son Ashikaga Yoshimitsu, who proved to be a more talented leader and politician. He realized that mere military might would never bring stability to the Ashikaga rule, so he sought to gain legitimacy by gaining civil offices in the imperial government. Despite not gaining any actual authority through them, he received much-needed political backing. It was him who moved the center of the bakufu from Kamakura to the Muromachi district in Kyoto in 1378 and during the 1380s continued to climb up the ranks of imperial officials. Yoshimitsu's biggest success came in 1392 when he managed to persuade the Southern Court to reconcile with the Northern branch of the imperial dynasty. He promised them that two family lines would switch on the throne, a promise which he then ignored, leading to the extinction of the Southern branch. Two years later, he was awarded the title of Grand Chancellor of State, the highest-ranking position in the civil government. Thus, he undisputedly became the most influential person of his era.

This merger of political and military power in the hands of the shōgun wasn't limited to ranks and titles. Yoshimitsu also integrated the bureaucracies of both governments, turning more and more civil prerogatives to the military governors, or shugo. For example, they were given the right to gather taxes. And in turn, members of the military aristocracy following his example started gathering ranks and titles appropriate to civil leaders, for example, the position of provincial governor. Furthermore, with rising questions of land disputes, more and more aristocrats started to group their estates in one place, making it easier to control and defend, while at the same time leaving the bulk of their inheritance to a single successor. This prevented splitting their family lands into smaller pieces. And indeed, those shugos who managed to gather great estates for themselves were the ones who benefited the most from the new regime, slowly turning into what modern historians call shugo-daimyō, meaning they were half military governors of the Kamakura and quasi-independent regional lords of the 14th century. While Yoshimitsu was still alive, he was still able to control them, but soon after his death in 1408, they started to ignore the edicts and orders of the Ashikaga shōguns.

Before his death, Yoshimitsu set two important precedents. Firstly, he abdicated in favor of his son, creating the title ex-shōgun, and as all authority remained in his hands, it was strikingly similar to the insei system of the late Heian period. Secondly, he reopened both trade and diplomatic relations with China, which was at the time ruled by the famous Ming dynasty. This revived the trade economy of Japan, allowing for an influx of coins, silk, and medicines, as well as Chinese culture in general through books, paintings, and similar products. More importantly, Yoshimitsu accepted the Chinese recognition of him as the "king of Japan." His gains were twofold; he gained wider Asian recognition both for himself and for Japan, and he was the primary benefiter of trade as it was taxed by the bakufu officials. This set up the precedent that the emperor shouldn't bother with foreign relations and instead leave those all up to the shōgun's will. Of course, many saw this as a usurpation of imperial prerogatives, but Yoshimitsu defended himself by explaining that he was merely shielding the emperor from facing the actuality of a letter of investiture and its disgrace. Some sources do mention that he was indeed planning to usurp the position of the Japanese monarch, but he died before actually trying anything, so historians aren't sure if those were really his intentions.

Whatever Yoshimitsu's actual plans were, after his death, the Muromachi bakufu was without a proper successor. As the central authority of the Ashikaga regime was wavering, the power of the local warlords was rising. Paired with that was the growing importance of Zen Buddhism, which first started spreading in the late 12th and early 13th centuries. It was brought from China, and its ideals were the perfect fit for the increasingly militaristic society of Japan. By the early 15th century, it became the most important religious faction as most samurais and shugo were following its word. Its teachings of simplicity, restraint, and discipline were the perfect ideals for a soldier, but it also preached confronting death without fear. These principles also spread into the Japanese culture, where they were displayed through the ideals of subdued taste, naturalism, elegant simplicity, and tranquil otherworldliness. Remnants of those ideas are still seen in modern Japanese culture. All of this made the Japanese society of the 15th and 16th century strikingly militaristic, and the bakufu was losing its capabilities to control the feudal lords. In 1441, the current shōgun was assassinated for trying to regain some of the lost authority, as local rebellions and skirmishes between the shugo became ever more common.

The state of things led to a full-out civil war in the 1460s. It erupted mainly because of the succession issues of the Ashikaga shōguns. Yoshimasa, shōgun at the time, was childless, so he adopted his own brother as his successor but surprisingly had a son in 1464. This drove a wedge between the brothers and the feudal lords that supported them. This hostility blew up in an open war known as the Ōnin War in 1467. It was fought throughout Japan, but the toughest fighting was around Kyoto. After a decade of bloody battles, the war subsided without a real victor, despite the fact that Yoshimasa was succeeded by his son Yoshihisa in 1473. The real result of the war was a disintegration of the bakufu's control over the feudal lords. They stayed nominal leaders of both the military and civil governments, but the warlords were now starting to deal with each other in their own struggle for power. And so, the period from 1467 to 1603 became known as the Sengoku period (Sengoku Jidai), or Age of the Warring States. From that point onward, the transformation of the military aristocracy from shugo to daimyō, a great feudal lord, was complete, as they were now pretty much independent and embroiled in almost never-ending warring among themselves with only nominal regard and respect for both the emperor and the shōgun.

A battle from the Ōnin War. Source: https://commons.wikimedia.org

Rather quickly, old clans and aristocratic families were displaced by capable leaders from smaller families, who rose to success through their cold-bloodedness and calculations. Most of these were former subordinates of the nobles who remained on their estates while their superiors were chasing after influence in the capital. Chaos ensued, everyone was fighting against everyone, fragile alliances would change quickly, and all sense of national unity was lost. Battles and armies grew larger, with up to 50,000 on one side. No longer were samurai the only soldiers on the field. However, they remained the superior force. Trained, mounted, and better equipped, they were rather similar to the medieval European knights. But the bulk of the fighting force was common foot soldiers known as ashigaru. They were supplied by their commanders and served under the military command of the samurai. And as they all fought as organized armies, battles were no longer fought one-on-one. During these bloody times, both the emperor and the shōgun were unable to gather enough authority to keep the feudal lords in line, but the governmental mechanisms of both the bakufu and the imperial administration survived, serving as the legal framework for the civil war.

By the mid-16th century, the war became a matter of everyday business. Despite that, the economy was growing. Many of the lords promoted economic expansion and trade as the size of their armies depended on the depth of their treasuries. This led to the cultivation of new lands, advances in agricultural techniques, and growth of the trade market. And as the most needed items were swords and armor, rudimentary forms of metalworking industries also developed. They were helped by foreign trade with China and Korea, where those items were exported alongside copper and sulfur. More importantly, in the 1540s, the first contacts with the Europeans, or to be more exact with the Portuguese, were made. Besides bringing Christianity, which never took much hold in Japan, they brought firearms which radically changed the nature of warfare. The feudal lords who were quick enough to adapt and adopt the new weapons started to gain the upper hand against their more traditional opponents. One such person was Oda Nobunaga, a daimyō from the Owari Province (part of the present-day Aichi Prefecture). As a perceptive strategist, he arose from a somewhat minor status to substantial power through a number of victories over rival lords. Because of that, in the 1560s, he got involved with the succession dispute of the bakufu on the request of the claimant Ashikaga Yoshiaki.

Being a very talented general, Nobunaga managed to capture Kyoto and install Yoshiaki as the new, and as it was going to turn out last, Ashikaga shōgun. But by that point, Nobunaga had become the most powerful daimyo, and he started to rule using Yoshiaki as a mere puppet. The new shōgun disliked that and used what was left of his influence and power to gain support against his former ally. This resulted in Yoshiaki's banishment from Kyoto in 1573, ending the Ashikaga shōgunate even though Yoshiaki retained his title until he officially resigned in 1588. In an attempt to tighten his hold over the country, Nobunaga started waging wars against other feudal lords, some being his former allies. At the same time, he also openly attacked Buddhist temples, which during the civil war grew their influence and power through their warrior monks. In these wars and attacks, he showed no mercy, killing captives and massacring the civil population if they got in his way. In 1575, it was Nobunaga who first used a substantial number of muskets to win a battle, the Battle of Nagashino, showing his ability to recognize the potential of the firearms that the Europeans brought to Japan. And by 1580, it seemed that Nobunaga was about to unify Japan once again as no other feudal lord was able to match his power. Yet his mission to reunite the Land of the Rising Sun was cut short in 1582 when one of his generals turned against him for unknown reasons. He caught Nobunaga unprepared, attacking him when he was traveling without guards. In his last defiant act, Nobunaga killed himself rather than having his head fall in the hands of his enemies.

European ships docked in a Japanese harbor. Source:
https://commons.wikimedia.org

It was no coincidence that two other daimyōs that went to fulfill his plans were his own vassals. The first to step forth to the stage was Toyotomi Hideyoshi. He was also an accomplished general and tactician who saw his opportunity in the death of his suzerain. He caught and punished the traitor, depicting himself as the protector of the Oda clan, and then used his gained power and influence to install Nobunaga's infant grandson as the head of the family. This made Hideyoshi the next leading daimyō in Japan. Another great lord that served under Nobunaga was Tokugawa Ieyasu, who slowly gained lands and power through his service to Nobunaga. As he was Hideyoshi's main rival at that point, they clashed in a struggle for power in 1584, but the campaign proved to be indecisive. Instead of pursuing the matter to the end, Ieyasu stepped down and accepted Hideyoshi as his superior. This allowed Hideyoshi to continue Nobunaga's dream of unification as he took down any other competitors one by one, often helped by Ieyasu. The last one to fall was the Go-Hōjō clan, unrelated to the previous Hōjō family, which fell in 1590. With this, Japan was unified, though only for a short time.

Both Nobunaga and Hideyoshi didn't become the shōgun, but the latter did take other courtly titles such as regent to legitimize his own rule. He treated Japan like his own domain, disregarding the traditional bureaucratic apparatus. And it proved to be a quite effective way to rule. He quickly gained a lot of power and wealth and then proceeded to invade Korea in 1592 and 1597. His goal was to conquer not only Korea but China as well. Despite some military victories and short-term territorial gains, both campaigns were total failures. This is why some historians believe that since he was a competent general, he would have known those attacks would be futile and that conquest wasn't his ultimate goal. Instead, they think he sent unreliable samurais and generals to die, but this interpretation remains questionable. Regardless, his hold over Japan was secured in the 1590s, but his legacy wasn't. He had an infant son, and to protect Toyotomi supremacy, Hideyoshi formed the Council of Five Elders (Go-Tairō) consisting of the five greatest feudal lords of the time to act as regents to his son when he died. Among them was Tokugawa Ieyasu, who after the fall of Go-Hōjō was given their territories in exchange for his. Hideyoshi did this to weaken his rather questionable ally, moving him farther away from the capital and forcing him to use time and resources in establishing his power base in the new domain.

The Battle of Sekigahara. Source: https://commons.wikimedia.org

However, instead of weakening him, this only strengthened him as he was awarded more land than he previously held which proved to be a great source of income and strength. There, Ieyasu chose the small fishing village of Edo as his new capital because of its central position in his newly gained territory. Under his rule, as well as of his successors, that little village grew into a true metropolis we today know as Tokyo. So, in 1598 when Hideyoshi died, Ieyasu was the most powerful daimyō, and for a year, he was kept in check by the other council members. Then one of the more experienced regents died, and Tokugawa Ieyasu saw his opportunity. Japan was once again in a civil war now divided between pro-Toyotomi and pro-Tokugawa factions. The sheer military power of Ieyasu attracted some former Toyotomi generals, while through his political capabilities, he managed to attract two of the other council members. The two groups clashed in the Battle of Sekigahara, located midway between Nagoya and Kyoto, and the Tokugawa forces emerged victorious. Afterward, no one could question his position as the leader of Japan. Ieyasu legitimized it by acquiring the position of shōgun in 1603, finally uniting Japan under one rule.

Thus, Oda Nobunaga, Toyotomi Hideyoshi, and Tokugawa Ieyasu were to become known as the three unifiers of Japan, military leaders who in succession took command over the lands and finally brought the Warring States period to an end. The differences in their characters are best represented with a famous Japanese saying which has those three leaders stumbling upon a songbird that refused to sing. Trying to resolve the matter, Nobunaga said, "I'll kill it if it doesn't sing." "I'll persuade it to sing," Hideyoshi replied. Ieyasu added, "I'll wait until it sings." These answers represent what was needed for unification to be accomplished—impulsiveness, self-confidence, and patience. With a combination of those, in 1603 Japan got its new shōgun family and peace, and it is when the Edo era and Tokugawa shōgunate started, pulling Japan out of the medieval times and into the modern age.

Chapter 6 – Japanese Society

Japanese society as it evolved through the centuries became ever more complex, more so than most other civilizations throughout history. This complexity comes from the fact that in this civilization the class hierarchy was sometimes parallel, like when it comes to the position of the warriors and nobles. It was also constantly changing through time, with huge local variations in medieval times as the country lacked true centralization. Another complicating factor was the familiar clan divisions. But in this chapter, an outline will be given of their society, with the most focus given to the feudalized and decentralized society of medieval Japan.

Japanese imperial banner. Source: https://commons.wikimedia.org

From the beginning of Japanese history, or at least the history of the Yamato, on top of all the people stood the monarch from the Yamato dynasty, a tradition continued even today. In the beginning, they were kings, but by the 8th century, they adopted the imperial title becoming heavenly sovereigns or tennō. In the early days, these monarchs were the true rulers of the country, with unquestionable authority, political influence, and even military might. It is through a combination of those that they managed to unite small kingdoms on the isles and actually create Japan. But as we have seen in previous chapters, their role over time became increasingly symbolic, with rare outbursts of some capable emperors who tried to recreate direct imperial rule. Nonetheless, no matter how symbolic their presence became, no warlord or noble dared to think about replacing the Yamato dynasty on the throne due to their religious role. As adopted from Chinese ideals, it was the ruler who was tasked with appeasing the gods for the good of the entire country. On top of that, they were mythologically connected to the gods that created Japan, and in their eyes, overthrowing the imperial dynasty would cause Japan to lose its divine protection. This long tradition is why even today, after 125 monarchs, Japan is officially ruled by the emperor in the constitutional parliamentary monarchy, despite not having any sovereignty.

In the ancient and classical times, it was the nobles who were the highest class beneath the emperor. They filled all the important positions in the government, actually helping the emperor rule the country. They were rich, educated, and owned large estates that funded their lifestyle. Despite sometimes leading armies, they weren't that connected to warfare, as in those eras war wasn't as common. Their power lay in the political influence they gained in the court. Through marriages, intrigues, and affairs, some of the nobles managed to become more powerful than even the emperors, usually seen in the position of regent some of them held. But as times changed and reliance on simple military strength became more important than political maneuvering, their importance dwindled. Their estates were absorbed by the warlords, the court lost its authority, and like the emperor, their position became more symbolic than actually relevant. Despite that, they were still held in high esteem because of their noble heritage, education, and inclination toward arts, with some of them managing to find a way to interfere with politics even in the medieval warrior dominated society.

Ashikaga Takauji, founder of the Ashikaga shōgunate. Source:
https://commons.wikimedia.org

From the 11th century onwards, society in Japan became increasingly militaristic as the importance of the warrior class rose. The first to gain influence was actually nobles who turned to war as their main focus for livelihood. It was these warriors with aristocratic descent who were able to combine their military strength and political influence to become either shōguns or shikkens, concentrating governmental authority in their hands and ruling instead of, or more precisely in the name of, the emperor. It was they who replaced the noble regents of the Heian period who were in control of the country. As such, they were at the top of the warrior class hierarchy. Below them were the so-called gokenin or shōgunal vassals. For their support, they received large estates and served in the bureaucracy of the bakufu, most often as estate stewards (jitō) and military governors (shugo). There was a relatively small number of gokenin, maybe up to 2,000 of them, but as they themselves had vassals and retainers, they were rather powerful and wealthy. And through this cascading feudal system, they brought a large number of soldiers into control of the shōgunate. In the late medieval period, during the civil war, it is from their ranks that the semi-autonomous feudal lords, or daimyo, arose. It is also worth noting that these high-ranking warriors were also usually well educated, as they also had to serve in the shōgunal administration.

Below the gokenin class were the samurai. Despite our present-day view on them as knightly warriors, it was actually a soldier class. They were mid-ranked in the social hierarchy and much more numerous than the gokenin. Samurai warriors also owned estates, though much smaller than the gokenin, had a decent income, and some of them were also educated. But their main focus was on fighting skills, and they were indeed the elite fighters in medieval Japan, serving primarily as cavalry. And though some of them were from noble descent, this wasn't a prerequisite to becoming a samurai. Similar to the gokenin, they also had their own vassals who were common foot soldiers. These were commoner warriors that served as the bulk of the fighting force. They were trained in combat but lacked all other education, had only small parcels needed to support their families, and were rather dependent on the other two warrior classes. Both them and the samurai spent most of their time on their own lands tending to them, unlike the gokenin who were often busy with developments in the capital and the government. And despite the idealized picture of Japanese warriors being loyal to a fault, during the 15th- and 16th-century civil wars, their allegiance was always questionable. Other aspects of Japanese warfare and soldiers will be discussed in another chapter.

Continuing down on the social hierarchy came farmers and peasants, known collectively as hyakushō. As the lower classes of Japanese society, they represented the tax base of the country, usually paying the land tax for the fields they were working on. There was also a class distinction between the farmers. Those who were wealthier and owned their own lands were called myoshu. They were local landholders who were rather independent, and they sometimes served for the estate (shoen) proprietors. Below them were kenin which literally translated means inferior people. They worked the land of the domain officials, estate owners, or in some cases even for myōshu farmers. Kenin had no rights to independently manage the lands they worked on nor freedom of movement. As they could be bought or sold and were usually linked to the land they worked on since they were a part of the estate inheritance, they are rather similar to the position of European feudal serfs. In the late medieval period, their social status started to change as kenin gained land rights as tenant farmers. Occasionally, some of the farmers had the opportunity to become warrior-farmers if their lords needed to fill up their armies. Warrior-farmers that showed enough skill and aptitude in fighting could then become part of the warrior class and work his way up the social hierarchy. Despite the fact that the living conditions and social freedoms of farmer sounds rather hard or unfair, it varied across Japan. It depended on local traditions and relations between the landowners and the farmers. In some cases, even kenin were treated as part of the extended family that controlled or owned the land.

At the bottom of the social hierarchy were the social outcasts. One group of them were called eta, or hereditary outcasts. These were members of families that worked on tasks that were seen as religiously impure, usually connected with working with the disposal or treatment of animals and animal hides, like butchers and tanners. Another group of social outcasts was hinin. Their position was a result of a social transgression, usually committing a crime. But one could also become hinin if their occupations were deemed socially improper, such as acting and other entertainment professions. Slaves, or nuhi, were also part of the lowest groups of Japanese society, but the information on them is actually rather questionable, in some aspects strikingly similar to kenin, and they never represented any significant percentage of the population. What is known is that by the end of the 16th century, elites regarded slavery as outdated and morally wrong, and in 1590, Toyotomi Hideyoshi officially banned slavery, though some forms of "forced labor" persisted through the next centuries.

So far, all of the social classes can be easily pinpointed in the hierarchy. But artisans' and merchants' positions in their society is rather hard to define. When we look at the theoretical division of the Japanese social order, it is clear that craftsmen and traders were at the bottom, just above the outcasts. This shouldn't be so surprising as this order was created in classical Japan when both of these economical fields were rather undeveloped. But as the medieval era was coming to an end, these two classes blossomed. Artisans became highly appreciated and sought-after as they were able to create objects that were either needed, like high-quality swords and muskets, or desired, like fine quality silk. On the other hand, traders were able to earn a lot of money, becoming rather influential in society, even though they were sometimes looked down upon. It is important to note that these classes rose in stature with the development of the entire Japanese economy in the late medieval period and were linked with the increased financial capabilities of the feudal lords who wanted to satisfy their desires through acquiring precious goods. And as artisans and merchants became more important, they started to gather in guilds (za) to create monopolies over the goods they made or sold.

The emergence of these two classes is indicative that the Japanese economy was booming from the Heian period onwards. The roots of this expansion were laid in agriculture. Technological advances such as the development of double cropping and the use of iron tools managed to increase farming production and created surplus that kickstarted local trade. Commerce proved to be a good source of income, and it was so desired by the feudal lords and nobles that they did their best to promote it. Gradually, merchants traveled across all of Japan, linking the entire country into one commercial network. This allowed the development of highly-skilled artisans who could create valuable items which weren't suitable for everyday use and everyone's pockets. With more items to offer and more money to buy, Japanese elites slowly started venturing into international trade, which prior to the late medieval times was sporadic and limited in scope. First, they connected with Korea, then with China, which was Japan's most important trading partner, and finally in the 16th century came the Europeans. This trade further developed the Japanese economy, allowing for an influx of copper coins which slowly started to replace the barter system. Gold and silver coins were also used but were more limited, as most of the population wasn't wealthy enough for it. This also shows that there were large financial differences in Japanese society, and only merchants and certain members of the elites were actually living comfortably. Farmers, artisans, and lower-class warriors remained poor, sometimes even resorting to social protests and revolts in an attempt to better their positions and livelihoods.

However, Japanese society was too rigid and hierarchal for these revolts to achieve any substantial gains. That rigidness can also be seen in the position of women in society. In the classical era, women were treated more equally. The best example of this was the fact that in those times there were several female monarchs that actually ruled Japan, be it with the title of a queen or an empress. That being said, they weren't really equal to men as they still held all the important offices and were generally in charge of the country, estate, and the family. Yet the arrival of Buddhism and Chinese thought, which was much more patriarchal than the Japanese culture, brought down the position of women. Some Buddhist schools saw women as impure because of menstruation and childbirth, and this reflected on their position in society. They were banned from inheriting estates and were in a way subordinate to their fathers and husbands. And as Japan was continually fractioned, women were often used to reinforce alliances through marriages or as hostages, making them merely a political chip. On the other hand, wives of warriors were in some cases trained in combat, and were not only able but expected to defend their home and domain while men were at war. And Buddhist temples did provide sanctuary to women who were trying to escape abusive marriages. It's noteworthy to point out that these examples were limited to women of higher status, so the image of the actual position of women in ancient Japanese society is still obscured by the lack of information.

An Asuka period mural depicting women. Source:
https://commons.wikimedia.org

Finally, the last quintessential part of the Japanese social structure were clans, which gave horizontal depth to an already quite vertically structured society. This division on kinships began in a time when the Yamato dynasty ruled over only their own kingdom, and though at one point the central government tried to suppress clans, they remained too important to be dissolved. With that being said, clans were only a part of the elite circles. Commoners usually remained limited to only their immediate relatives as they simply weren't rich enough to establish such a complex social structure. To aristocrats, clans were one of the most important parts of life. First of all, not all clans were equal. Some were large and influential, like the Fujiwara or Minamoto, while others remained smaller, though still respectable. And some clans were specialized for certain tasks, like warfare or administration. Despite the mutual respect the clans had among themselves, they were almost constantly in conflict with one another, fighting for supremacy. In a society like this, loyalty to one's clan was supreme, in some cases coming before the loyalty to the country or the emperor. Clans also played an important role in religious life as well, as most of them had their own temples and ancestor cults. And on top of the clan hierarchy was the head of the family, who commanded all other members of the clan as he wished. It was also possible to adopt someone into the clan, which was usually either to bolster the clan's strength or as a token of appreciation for someone's service.

Loyalty was truly appreciated in medieval Japanese society, which was quite divided and distinctly hierarchical. It both reflected the development of Japanese culture and history while at the same time affecting them as well. Even today, remnants of these divisions and traditions are seen in the Japanese civilization. The highly structured and hierarchical system is most obvious in modern-day corporate life in Japan where just through greetings and bowing you can see who is who's superior.

Chapter 7 – Warriors of Ancient Japan

As Japanese culture and society became militaristic in its nature, warriors became one of the most important parts of this civilization. So, without understanding them, one cannot understand Japan and its history. This is especially important because modern misconceptions presented through movies and books strongly influence our vision of medieval Japanese soldiers. The simplest example of this is that one often thinks of all Japanese warriors as samurai and all samurai as warriors. As we have seen in the previous chapter, the samurai was a warrior class, but many of them also turned to the arts. And actually, that very term became widespread only as the civil war was slowly coming to an end and with the unification of Japan under the Tokugawa regime.

The most common term used to name warriors, in general, was bushi, literary translated as the men of the martial arts. It became prevalent in the Nara period in the 8th century, predating the word samurai for about 200 years. And when the word samurai was introduced, it was specifically used to distinguish warriors in service of the nobles. In the Kamakura period, samurai were the ones who were given an official rank by the shōgun or the imperial court. It was only in the later medieval period that this term indicated soldiers of a comparatively high social status. On the other hand, bushi always remained a term for warriors in general, but in later periods, they were all considered to be part of "warrior houses," or buke in Japanese. These grew from warrior bands, or bushidan, which served the nobles in the provinces, helping officials preserve peace and order. Over the centuries, buke became a word synonymous with bushi and began to refer to the entire warrior class. And warrior leaders, who commanded both the greatest armies and largest domains, grew ever more powerful during the Sengoku period, eventually becoming known as daimyō, meaning "great name." During that era, the warrior class became the pinnacle of Japanese society, if not in theory, then at least in practice.

It was in the era of daimyōs that the warfare in Japan became how most modern people envision it. During the classical era, wars were fought by the conscripted peasants who were led by nobles on the battlefield. But as the central government weakened, the conscription wavered. That left the nobles in need of armies who then had to pay for their services, actually creating the warrior class. But these were still relatively small armies, numbering in hundreds or at the utmost a few thousand people. And in that early medieval period, pretty much all of the people on battlefields were trained soldiers, and battles were more procedural. They were often fought by small armies in which individual soldiers broke off into one-on-one duels. In some cases, the battles were even decided by the duels of the two army generals themselves. But as the fighting grew fiercer and the stakes higher, and as Japan descended into the civil war, generals realized that relying on the warrior class wasn't enough. They once again started conscripting peasants for their armies, but now they were led by the trained samurai warriors, who were indeed the elite warriors of Japan. Armies grew larger, numbering up to 50,000 men, and they were better organized. Tactics also became more important as the battles became massive, no longer a matter of individual duels but of well-synchronized actions of thousands. And with that, the number of casualties grew as well, making the Sengoku period probably the bloodiest in Japanese history after World War II.

Sengoku period battle. Source: https://commons.wikimedia.org

However, despite the gritty reality of warfare in which the samurai showed little mercy to each other, they did have a philosophy and a code of conduct guiding them. Inspired by Chinese Confucian thoughts, some of the most important samurai ideals were loyalty and honor. It was a matter of personal and familial reputation, fulfilling one's duty toward both his superiors and inferiors. They were also expected to be well-mannered and dressed properly, as any imperfection would be seen as a sign of a personal character flaw. Another important part of the samurai life was marriage, as the

Confucian patriarchal ideal saw it as a necessity for the harmony of society. If a samurai disobeyed the codes of conduct, he was expected to end his own life. It was done through a ritual called seppuku, or as it is also known harakiri. Committed by ripping open one's own stomach, seppuku was seen as a way to restore both personal and familial honor, as the abdomen was thought to be the residing place of the human soul. This ritual suicide was also done when ordered by the samurai's feudal lord when a warrior failed his task or duty. One step further was the practice of junshi. When a samurai lord performed seppuku or was killed in battle, in some occasions, he was followed in death by his own retainers as a sign of their loyalty.

Of course, these ideals weren't always followed, and there are many examples of disloyalty and cruelness among the samurai. But in later periods, the view on samurai became romanticized, and these virtues were the focus of their image. This was further strengthened under the Tokugawa regime when the set of rules for samurai were compiled. That guide for the Japanese warriors became known as bushido or the way of the warrior. It was also in that era that a romanticized image of the sword-wielding samurai became predominant. In reality, early samurais most commonly used bows and arrows which they usually fired while riding on horseback. Because of that, archery and horsemanship remained an important skill that the samurai trained in. They also used pole weapons like naginata, which was a wooden or metal pole with a curved single-edged blade on the end and looked like a combination of a sword and a spear. It was between 1.5 to 3 m (5 to 10 ft) long. Naginata was later replaced by yari, which was a plainer spear, 4.5 to 6.5 m (15 to 21 ft) long. Of course, most samurais wore swords, and not just one but usually two, a longer and a shorter one. But they were mostly used as a last resort or for dueling to settle personal differences out of combat.

Nonetheless, those swords were highly praised and seen as a class status symbol by the samurai. This is why by the late medieval period the craftsmanship of Japanese sword makers became astonishing. They became considerably adept in using folded and layered steel to create high-quality blades from fewer amounts of quality iron ore. This was done because Japan lacked the resources of iron and it had to be imported. This is how the samurai became known for their superior katana swords. But actually, the katana was just one type of sword they used, and it was among the last to develop, in the late 13th and early 14th centuries. It was about 60 cm (2 ft) long and suitable for dueling. On the other hand, tachi swords were older, dating back to the 10th century and were longer, approximately 90 cm (3 ft) long. And with the introduction of katanas, they were made more as regalia than as real combat weapons. Tantō and wakizashi were short swords or daggers, with the main differences being their length (tantōs were between 15 to 30 cm, or 6 to 12 in., and wakizashis were between 30 and 60 cm, or 12 to 24 in.) and that the tantō didn't have a handguard. All these types had their own varieties, but what they all had in common was that they were curved backward.

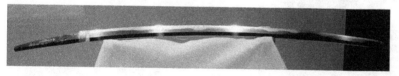

14th-century katana. Source: https://commons.wikimedia.org

Unlike European knights, the samurai didn't usually carry handheld shields. They did use mantlets, wooden barriers stuck in the ground that were used as protection from enemy projectiles. They also sometimes used a long piece of fabric draped over their backs so that it could catch arrows. This was the most effective during rapid maneuvers and charges that caused those pieces of fabric to billow up like a bag. It also proved useful for messengers who had no other way to defend themselves from their pursuers. But of course, the main type of defense was armor. The Japanese preferred lamellar armor, known as ō-yoroi, made from small leather or iron scales, often even combining the two to increase protection and decrease weight. They proved to be more effective and lighter than European chainmail of that era. In the late medieval period, a simplified version of ō-yoroi appeared, called haramaki. It was cheaper and often used for foot soldiers. At the same time, wealthier samurai were slowly starting to transition to dō, a type of plate armor which was necessitated by the arrival of firearms. Samurai also wore helmets, or kabuto, made out of sheets of iron or steel with flaps at the sides and back. That way they offered protection for the neck as well. Armors and helmets for the samurai had more than just a simple protective use. They were often colored and highly adorned with regalia and ornaments through which they showed their allegiances, inspired their fellow warriors, and instilled fear to the enemy. Together with swords, they were part of a family's heirlooms and often passed through generations of samurai families.

A Kamakura period armor and helmet. Source:
https://commons.wikimedia.org

During the civil war, when armies grew in size, the samurai weren't alone on the battlefield anymore. They were in fact heavily outnumbered by common foot soldiers known as ashigaru (light of foot). These warriors usually lacked any complex military training and were supplied by their feudal lords. They wore simpler armors and conical helmets. Though they were usually made out of iron, sometimes they also wore leather equipment. The ashigaru were usually armed with pole weapons, usually yari and sometimes naginata, as they required less training to use proficiently. They were also used as archers, which to a degree diminished archery in the eyes of the samurai. By the end of the 16th century, some smaller numbers of ashigaru were armed with muskets as well, since firearms became more common on the battlefield. These troops were usually seen as less worthy and more replaceable than the samurai, who required years of harsh training to achieve their knowledge of both martial arts and strategy. Another type of combatant that appeared in medieval Japan was the sōhei or warrior monks. They started to appear in times of insecurity as a protection for the major Buddhist temples, and they proved to be formidable foes as they were both well-armed and skilled fighters. Despite being called monks, not all sōhei were part of the monastic order at the temples they served.

A warrior monk or sōhei. Source: https://commons.wikimedia.org

For that reason, it wasn't uncommon for sōhei to become a menace to society, robbing the commoners and expanding the lands belonging to the temples. Many imperial and shōgunal leaders fought hard against them. The last type of soldiers, if one can call them that, were the shinobi. To Westerners, they are more familiar as the ninja. In a romanticized view of the past, these were skilled acrobats, dressed in all black, climbing castle walls and assassinating their targets. They were the opposite of samurai ideals. However, the truth about them is much more mundane. Shinobi dressed to best suit with their surroundings, and their main task was espionage and sabotage, though they did sometimes assassinate people if needed. And they weren't the exact opposite of the valorous samurai, as they were hired and used by almost all daimyōs. By the very end of the medieval period, ninjutsu, the art of covert and guerrilla warfare, was slowly becoming integrated as a part of a samurai's training. The number of tools and weapons used by them is great, from katanas and throwing daggers and stars, to grappling hooks and smoke bombs. The secret to their success was adaptability. However, their usefulness was a short period, from the 14th to early 17th centuries, when Japan was in disarray. After that, the shinobi slowly died out.

That fate was shared by many other Japanese warriors after Tokugawa's victory. Many samurais were left without their masters, becoming ronin (floating men). Yet the militant spirit of the Japanese civilization endured. It was saved by the fact that the Tokugawa regime was still a shōgunate, a military government, which praised its roots and traditions, even though in later periods they presented that past in a very distorted and biased way. Thus, warriors remained an important part of the Japanese way of life even during their peacetime.

Chapter 8 – Religious Life in Japan

As in many other ancient societies, religion played an important role in the history of Japan. It was religion that shaped its art and culture, fostered connections with mainland Asia, and influenced the development of Japanese thought. Without religion, the Japanese civilization couldn't be understood, especially if we consider the fact that the emperor or tennō was first and foremost their religious leader and only secondly and sporadically their secular monarch. That connection comes from the indigenous religion of the Japanese known as Shinto.

Traditional Shinto temple. Source: https://commons.wikimedia.org

Literally translated it means "the way of the god," and it is based around worshiping a multitude of gods or deities known as kami. According to tradition, there are over eight million kami, and their nature is neutral. If worshipped properly, they are benevolent; if not, they turn destructive. This is why the ritual practices that include purifications, food offerings, dances, and festivals honoring the deities are central to Shinto. They are done to appease the kami. And central to it is the emperor, whose main religious task is to keep the entire country in favor of the gods. Another important aspect of kami worship is family and ancestors. Though there are Shinto temples, it isn't uncommon for families to have their own home shrines where they would pay respects to the deceased members of their families who would sometimes even be considered as kami themselves. These aspects show a strong Chinese influence on the Japanese religion, which predates the introduction of Buddhism. Shinto is also a very communal religion, which is exhibited through festivals and public rituals where all members of the community would pray for everyone's wellbeing. And as kami were also connected to nature itself, the ancient Japanese respected their surroundings, thinking that some of the deities were living in things like forests and rivers. The highest veneration of the natural world was reserved to the mountains which were thought to have the strongest connection both to the kami and their ancestors, which is why temples and shrines were often built on them.

What especially separates Shinto from most other religions in the world is the fact that it has no core sacred texts or founders. The traditions were "unified" and standardized only in the late medieval period with many local variations and customs. Yet there was a centralized state cult linked directly to the emperor and the imperial family. The tennō wasn't only a high priest, but through mythology, he was also a direct descendant of the creator gods that formed Japan. This is what kept the Yamato dynasty on the throne despite the fact that most of the later emperors held no real political power. Since the ancestors of their monarchs were gods, that meant that both the imperial family and their country were chosen and favored by the gods, making them impervious to outside attacks and superior to other civilizations. This notion was only heightened after the Mongol invasions in the 13th century. Nevertheless, Shinto remained an open religion itself without disregarding other traditions or beliefs. This is why when Buddhism arrived there weren't any major turmoil or conflicts.

12th-century Buddhist temple. Source: https://commons.wikimedia.org

On top of that, Buddhism itself isn't a very aggressive religion. Originating in India, it traveled through China to Japan. And since its arrival in the mid-6th century, it grew quickly, mostly thanks to the patronage of the early Yamato kings. The main Buddhist teachings of gaining enlightenment (nirvana) and liberation from suffering through meditation and morality of one's actions (karma) were rather compatible with Shinto. It is also important to point out that Buddhism had many different versions and teachings, both in Japan and the rest of Asia. So already by the classical Nara period, there were more than six different Buddhist schools in Japan, all preaching different paths toward nirvana. The first of those was founded by the Chinese Buddhist masters that migrated to Japan to spread their religion. Later on, new schools were founded by Japanese monks who went to China to gain sufficient knowledge and practice to create their own teachings. It was only in the late 12th and early 13th centuries that monks who were educated in Japan could attain the rank of a Buddhist master. Though their ideas and teachings continued to be influenced by the religious developments in China, by that time, it became a common practice of the Buddhists in Japan to rely on temples and monks and established rituals to attain the enlightenment.

Zen master Dōgen. Source: https://commons.wikimedia.org

Yet for some monks, like famed Eisai Zenji and Dōgen Zenji, this approach was wrong. It was too reliant on others to achieve peace and nirvana, and it made people too dependent on monks. Those two separately traveled to China in the late 12th and early 13th centuries, bringing Zen Buddhism to Japan for the first time. First becoming Zen masters in Japan, they then preached that attaining nirvana could be realized through everyday life, by relying on oneself and more traditional practices such as meditation. This type of Buddhism was more monastic in its nature, and in the beginning, it wasn't as popular. However, the strict and hierarchical nature of Zen schools became more and more popular among the rising warrior class, and through the patronage of the Kamakura bakufu, the Hōjō family, and later on the Ashikaga shōgunate, it became the most influential

Buddhist teachings. Its importance rose significantly when Zen monks started to participate in the shōgunal government from the 14ᵗʰ century onwards, as their temples became part of the state administrative system. The influence of Zen thought on Japanese culture became immense, from reintroducing the ideals of a moderate way of life to simpler things such as drinking tea.

That influence wasn't limited only to the Zen schools as Buddhism in general permeated Japanese art, their way of thinking, and civilization in general. And despite the supremacy achieved by Zen Buddhism, other schools never ceased to exist, and all of the temples continued to operate through the centuries, continuing and, in some cases, evolving their teachings and traditions. This coexistence was also eased by the fact that most of the Japanese continued to practice Shinto ceremonies, making their actual religion, in essence, a mixture of Shinto and Buddhist beliefs and customs. This was achievable as Buddhism never negated the existence of gods, and both religions had a close connection with the state as well as certain similar ideals. For example, both religions were focused on worldly problems like poverty and illness, while death was only a transition, not a permanent "end." And through Confucian influence, both Shinto and Buddhism saw the family as one of the sources of religious activity and respected their ancestors. And despite Zen teachings, most Buddhists and Shintoists relied on prayers, invocations, festivals, and ritual offerings to achieve their goals. Thus, despite never actually fusing into one religion, Buddhism and Shintoism remained inextricably linked. Even today most Japanese practice the syncretism of Buddhism and kami worship known as shinbutsu-shūgō.

However, there was one major difference between Shintoism and Buddhism. The latter was introduced by the Chinese, who brought literacy with them. As such, the earliest forms of education was tightly connected with Buddhist monks. In the classical period, education was only available to the nobles, who could afford to pay teachers, and those learning to become Buddhist priests. But as

Buddhism started to gain wider popularity in the early middle ages, temples started opening schools for a broader population. However, literacy was in general still rather low and confined to aristocrats and the rising samurai class. In 1432, the Ashikaga School (Ashikaga Gakkō), which is originally thought to be founded in the ninth century, was restored, and it was connected with the ruling shōgunal family. And even though it was the first secular school, it was still headed by a Buddhist monk at the time of its creation. The curriculum was focused on military strategy and Confucian philosophy, as the students were supposed to be mainly from the warrior class. By the mid-16th century, this school had over 3,000 students from all over Japan. The education given in Ashikaga Gakko was of such quality that even the Jesuit missionary Francis Xavier expressed his admiration for it, which wasn't common for Christians to do for the population they were trying to convert.

Christianization of the Japanese in the 16th century was at best moderately successful. Missionaries, most commonly from the Jesuit and Franciscan order, were confronted by cultural differences and worldviews. The Japanese had a hard time accepting the idea that only those who accepted Christianity would be saved, meaning that their dead ancestors would be condemned for eternity no matter what. Despite that, it is estimated that by 1580 around 130,000 Japanese were converted in a population that numbered at least 8 to 10 million people. This number was heightened due to some of the converted feudal lords forcing their subjects to convert as well. The helping factor for the missionaries was the backing of Oda Nobunaga and Toyotomi Hideyoshi. They saw the opportunity to use Christians to oppose the mighty Buddhist temples which had grown too powerful to control, as well as to boost their economy by trading with the Europeans. But as unification was coming to a close, Christianity was seen as a threat to the unity and national identity of the Japanese. So, in 1587, Hideyoshi turned back on his stance toward them and ordered all missionaries to leave Japan. This order was enacted only sporadically, and Christian missionaries continued to work. When Tokugawa Ieyasu took control over Japan, he was tolerant toward the Christians to maintain friendly relations with the Western merchants. Yet later the Tokugawa bakufu started to shut off Japan from foreign influences, and governmental policies turned against the Christians. The shogunate officially banned Christianity in 1614 and issued another statement calling for the expulsion of all Christian missionaries. That same year, the shogunate began the systematic persecution of Christians. Buddhist temples were given the responsibility of verifying that a person, via the temple guarantee system (terauke seido), was not a Christian. By 1639, they had killed at least 1,000 Christians, expelled at least another 13,000 local Christians to Manila, and effectively ended the open practice of Christianity. It only survived by going underground.

For what has been said, it is obvious how important religion was for the history of Japan. Both Buddhism and Shintoism were close with the state, from ideological backgrounds to administration. And temples were crucial for spreading literacy, education, and knowledge in general. Not to mention that religious traditions were in part one of the many roots of the national identity of the Japanese. It bound both local and national communities through common practices and rituals and gave the Japanese their common mythical roots. And both Buddhism and Shintoism were, in fact, part of everyday life in ancient Japan, leaving an unquestionable mark on the evolution of its culture and civilization.

Chapter 9 – Japanese Culture

Like all other great civilizations, Japan created a unique culture. It was a mixture of indigenous traditions, Chinese and Buddhist influences, and, in later periods, warrior ideals. These combined together weaved a culture we know today, connecting various astonishing artworks and writings through the ages into one constantly growing and evolving yet still coherent system. And it is important to shed some light on that as well, as too many times when thinking about ancient Japan, we focus only on the wars and soldiers, intrigues and politics, and on generals and emperors. In fact, Japanese history is much more than just that.

Yamato-e style painting. Source: https://commons.wikimedia.org

One of the most recognizable forms of Japanese art is paintings. Developed with heavy Chinese influence, it can be divided into two major groups. The older group is the so-called kara-e (Chinese-style picture). First introduced in the Nara period, it drew its style directly from Chinese art. These are usually more monochromatic, using either just black and white or different shades of the same color. Another distinguishable detail is that the landscape is more mountainous, looking more like mainland China than Japan. The other, younger group formed in the late Heian period and blossomed later in the medieval era, adding more vibrant and thicker colors while still representing the more gently rolling landscapes that characterize Japan. It is known as Yamato-e (Japanese-style picture). Of course, both of these styles evolved and changed over the years, influenced by historical developments. For example, Heian painters often focused on courtly themes, romances, and in general had more gentle themes. With the rise of the warrior class, painters turned toward representations of military conquests, war epics, and in general more masculine and martial types of art. By the 16th century, some painters also started depicting the everyday life of the different social classes. However, landscapes and religious themes remained a constant in ancient Japanese paintings. And unlike most European paintings, Japanese artists usually painted on silk or paper scrolls of various sizes, as well as wooden and paper doors and walls.

As such, paintings were used to decorate a wide array of places from private homes to palaces and courts as well as temples. In contrast to that, statues were usually found in temples. Most commonly made out of wood and in some cases bronze or clay, these sculptures customarily had Buddhist themes. The early sculptors from the Asuka period leaned toward unrealistic and mythical representations of their subjects with a feel of steadiness and godliness. Through the centuries, there was a slow shift toward a more human form grounded in realism. Sculptures were given a more dramatic feel with a more direct manifestation of emotions and movement. Despite that, serenity was still quite present. With the end of the Kamakura bakufu, realism was further enhanced to a measure where it became exaggerated realism. An example of that was the practice of using crystal insets for eyes (gyokugan, or "jewel eyes"). By the medieval era, it also became common to paint and decorate wooden sculptures, giving them a more vivid presence. In the earlier periods, sculptors were employed usually by temples themselves or in some cases the emperors, but in later medieval times, the patronage shifted toward the members of the higher warrior class. In that period, there is both a decline in the quality and quantity of statues, but also in some cases, those patrons also requested portrait statues of themselves, shifting slightly from the Buddhist themes.

12ᵗʰ-century wooden statue. Source: https://commons.wikimedia.org

Buddhism also influenced another more practical art form which is architecture. In the earliest periods, Japanese builders erected simple structures from unpainted and untreated wood with simple ornamentation. With the arrival of Buddhism, Chinese influence started to shift these characteristics toward colored and treated wood, with more decorations and higher and bigger structures. Tall multistory pagodas became the common type of building for Buddhist temples. But through time, Japanese architects realized that earthquakes were rather common in their country and employed the use of penetrating tie beams which gave structures more sturdiness and was also a simple way of decorating columns and beams. They also started using thicker woodwork which was more durable and imposing. And with the spreading of Zen ideas and the establishment of a militaristic society, in the middle ages, Japanese builders once again turned toward a more simplistic style of ornamentation. When Zen Buddhism arrived from China, it brought bell-shaped windows to Japanese architecture. By that time, pagodas were slowly going out of fashion. Zen principles also changed the gardens, introducing sand or gravel to replace water found in ponds and lakes, which were common in the earlier periods. In contrast to Buddhist architecture, Shinto shrines remained small and simple, usually built to resemble old granaries. The most recognizable aspect of Shinto architecture was the temple gate which, though simple in structure with two horizontal beams, played an important religious role as the gateway into the sacred precinct. Today that gate, known as torii, is accepted as a worldwide symbol of Shintoism.

Traditional Shinto torii gate. Source: https://commons.wikimedia.org

Both of these religions were also connected with other performing arts. Shinto priests performed kagura, the music and dance of the kami. It had various local variations, but it was at some point done by the emperor himself in the royal court. In Buddhist rituals, it was common to use ritual chanting, dances, and various music. However, both music and dancing were common in non-religious forms. From the Nara period came the gagaku, musical tradition, and bugaku, dance tradition, which were performed at court. Despite being secular in nature, as these were connected with the court, they still had some religious connotations and as such were occasionally performed in both Shinto shrines and Buddhist temples. Like in other aspects of Japanese culture, the rise of the military class also affected the music. By the 12th century, recitals that told stories about battles and heroes accompanied by music became rather popular. Combining Buddhist chanting with court music, these were collectively known as heikyoku. These retellings of warrior tales were later expanded into reenactments by a small number of actors but still retained the form of a dramatic song and dance. These were known as kōwakamai and served as a precursor to the theater. Another form of a song influenced by the rise of the warrior class was the "banquet song," or enkyoku. As these were played at feasts and celebrations, they were less serious and a livelier version of music.

Late medieval musicians. Source: https://commons.wikimedia.org

Besides these, there were many variations of local or regional musical traditions and dances which historians collectively call folk music, yet not all of them are well known and studied. However, most of the music of ancient Japan was played on traditional instruments. The most common were the bamboo flute (shakuhachi), double reed flute (hichiriki) which sounds like the modern-day clarinet, 13-string zither-like instrument known as koto, a three-string plucked lute (shamisen), as well as kokyū, a bowed lute. It is clear that most of these were influenced by the Chinese tradition, though they were developed to suit the Japanese culture. The Japanese also had two different styles of drums. The large one is known as taiko, which is laid on the ground and beaten with thick sticks. The other style is called tsuzumi, which are handheld lacquered wooden drums in an hourglass shape. All of these instruments created various notes and rhythms, but in traditional Japanese music, silence (ma) or the space between the notes was also important. This was also seen in dances when performers paused between their movements. Such silences or pauses were seen as an integral part of the music while serving as a practical tool to heighten the audience's anticipation.

Dance and music evolved into theater which had two styles, noh and kyogen, and appeared in the late 14th and early 15th centuries. Both of these styles put an emphasis on mime and stylized dances and songs to retell a story, with a focus on human emotions. One of the characteristics of those types of acting was the use of certain established gestures and movements to signal to the audience about the actions and transitions that didn't actually happen onstage, like long travels. Noh was a serious dramatic form with plays retelling stories of gods and demons, and warriors and court ladies, and it was grounded in Buddhist sensibilities. In contrast to noh, kyogen was performed by amateurs who improvised comic reliefs acts, usually in between scenes or before a noh play. Thus, both styles often came in a package.

This early Japanese theater used both poems and prose, and they often told already known stories, many of them already told through literature. The earliest recorded stories were found in two chronicles *Kojiki* and *Nihon Shoki*. Written in the early 8th century, they combined both historical events and mythological tales. In that very same century, the first poems were recorded. Known as kanshi, they were written in the Chinese style with Chinese characters. By the Heian period, waka, or Japanese poems, having originated in the

Kojiki, experienced a revival; these poems had aristocratic themes and values. Like all later poems, it also had a strict formulaic structure with a certain number of lines and syllables. In the middle ages, a new type of poem was created known as renga. It followed a similar pattern as waka, but it linked their verses into long stanzas. This allowed for more variety and led to the decline of waka in the 15th century. However, from shorter renga sections, a more internationally famous type of style arose, the haiku poem.

As for prose, it also developed in the medieval times, branching from chronicles into several other forms, with more warrior and worldly themes. One of the most widespread styles was the diary or memoir, which were recollections of certain events or travels. Similar to them were war tales (gunki monogatari). These narrated glorious battles, victories and defeats, and retold heroic feats. These reinforced warrior ethics and were very popular with the ruling warrior class of the medieval era. Essays, or zuihitsu (following the writing brush), were also written. These were diverse treatises or random thoughts, created from personal observations about nature and people and written with no specific structure in mind. It should be pointed out that literature was written almost exclusively by aristocrats and Buddhist monks. And among them, calligraphy was also popular. Introduced by the Chinese, in the early periods it was done with both Chinese characters (kanji) and style, but later many started using the Japanese writing system (kana) and developed an indigenous Japanese style. Calligraphy was rather popular in both the noble court as well as among the samurai. Warriors praised it as it required calmness, discipline, and precision, which is why it was also linked with Zen Buddhism in the medieval period.

In both calligraphy and other manners of writing, it was common to use both Chinese and Japanese characters. However, that doesn't mean that the Japanese were writing in the Chinese language. Instead, they used Chinese characters, or rather their pronunciation, to write down their own language in its own form and structure. That being said, it should be stressed that Chinese and Japanese languages, despite sounding similar to the untrained ear of the Westerner, have no common roots or connections. They are different languages. For this reason, the use of kanji was rather complicated, along with the added difficulty that it had two ways of pronunciation. This pushed Japanese scholars to develop kana, which was, in essence, a simplified version of the kanji characters with specifically designated syllable sounds linked with them. This made it much simpler to use for the Japanese. But throughout Japanese history, even today, both kana and kanji remain in use, both separately and in various combinations.

So far, most of the cultural achievements of ancient Japan were in various degrees influenced by the Chinese civilization, yet they were adopted and evolved into something that was more Japanese in its essence. Unfortunately, when it comes to natural sciences like medicine, mathematics, and astrology, the indigenous Japanese contributions were more than limited. In medicine, the traditional Chinese idea of a vital force known as qi (or ki in Japanese) was the main base of treatment. Thus, the focus was on the entire body and person, not singular symptoms. This was supplemented with the Buddhist ideas of karmic diseases from past lives. So, treatment was both spiritual and physical. The former was done through things like prayers or ritual cleansings, while the latter was done by using various plant and animal ointments, potions, creams, and similar concoctions. Japanese healers also practiced acupuncture as a way to unblock ki energy. Astronomy, another science, was used mostly for timekeeping and the calendar, which was based on the Chinese calendar and their astronomical practices and technologies. In mathematics, the Chinese system was in use throughout the ancient era; only after Tokugawa's unification did local mathematicians develop the Japanese mathematical system. Considering that the Japanese society was more military orientated, it isn't surprising that there weren't any considerable scientific breakthroughs in this era, but the Japanese did have a long tradition of making complex mechanisms, which is obvious from the rather quick adoption of firearms production. This can still be seen to this day as the Japanese are the leaders in robotics technology.

Similar to science, philosophy wasn't one of the important subjects to the ancient Japanese. The furthest extent was the adoption of Confucian ideals, as seen in the importance of propriety and retaining harmony with heaven. To the Japanese that meant it was important to act in a morally and socially acceptable manner, leading to a seemingly strict society. Another ideal of the Confucian teachings was the importance of family and familial piety, which heavily influenced the development of the clan system. However, this permeated the lower layers of society as well. In the basic family unit, or ie (house), the oldest man was the head of the household and held the highest responsibilities. But as idleness was frowned upon, everyone in the home was expected to do some work, regardless of age, gender, or even socioeconomic status. Women were tasked with maintaining the household while children were taught how to perform various housework usually early on in their life. Most of a child's education, especially for the lower classes, came from their parents. The actual houses in which they lived were usually small, simple, and adaptable structures, due to the volatile conditions of the climate and natural disasters. They were furnished in a simplistic manner with few pieces of furniture. They most commonly used tatami woven floor mats, zabuton cushions for sitting, short tables, and futon mattresses placed on the ground for sleeping. Heat and lighting typically came from a central fireplace.

That fireplace was also used for cooking. Traditional Japanese cuisine consisted of seafood, marine vegetation, seasonal vegetables, and rice, which constituted the bulk of the meal. The meat was seen as impure because of religious stipulations. So, the nobles and monks avoided it, while commoners and lower rank warriors consumed it more regularly. To supplement the lack of meat, soybean products were used. For example, they used miso, a nutritious grain and soybean paste made with rice or barley, and tofu. Common spices were soy sauce, ginger, wasabi (Japanese horseradish), and sansho, a powder made from ground seedpods of the prickly ash tree. During the medieval period, it was common for the nobles and higher classes to eat twice a day, while commoners, because of their more physically exhausting work, ate up to four times per day. Influenced by Chinese tradition, the Japanese consumed their meals with chopsticks, usually made from wood. One of the modern-day staples of Japanese cuisine is, of course, rice wine known as sake. Its roots can be found in the classical era, but it gained its popularity in the middle ages. This beverage was at first consumed at celebrations and festivals, and in later periods it became an everyday drink. It was also customary to drink tea after the meal. However, this tea was prepared and drank differently than in the famous tea ceremonies.

More art than anything else, these ceremonies of tea drinking were introduced with the arrival of Zen Buddhism, despite the fact that tea had been drunk in Japan since the 8th century. The ritual of preparing tea became known as chanoyu, meaning hot water for tea, or chado, the way of tea. It had very precise steps which were required to prepare a perfect sip of tea, as well as a dubious number of specialized utensils used in its preparations. Because of this, mastering the ceremony took years of practice and gathering of different tools. These ceremonies were usually reserved for the upper class. However, drinking tea in such a manner wasn't just showing off one's knowledge and discipline. It also had a more spiritual role. Shinto and Buddhist ideals were connected with it, as it reflected harmony and calmness. For that reason, tea practitioners do not prefer to define their gatherings as "ceremonies" because that word implies a stiffness that they try to eliminate through their meditative and religious concepts of tea preparation.

Modern Japanese tea ceremony. Source: https://commons.wikimedia.org

Despite that, the ancient Japanese culture embodied strictness and stiff rules which can also be seen through the hairstyles worn. They reflected one's age, status, and sexuality. For example, samurais wore their hair in a topknot which was, at the start, a pragmatic need of a warrior as loose hair could be pulled in battle. Later on, it started to represent belonging to a warrior class in general. Up to the 16th century, women kept their hair long and straight. Afterward, they slowly began to put their hair up and decorate them with various combs, pins, and other ornaments. Cosmetics were used by both men and women on a regular basis. Pale skin was seen as the most desirable, so many women used face powder known as oshiroi to whiten their faces. And contrary to present-day standards, blackened teeth were a common trend. It was done by an oxidized liquid which also preserved the teeth. This practice was called ohaguro, and it was used mostly by women, though in the late medieval period, it became popular among men as well. The clothing they wore was also indicative of one's class and profession. For example, in the Kamakura period, the typical warrior uniform consisted of a hunting jacket (kariginu) and a cloak (suikan). Formal attire worn by women included a robe (uchiki), skirt-trousers (hakama), and a silk garment with short sleeves (kosode). As for the kimono, the most famous part of traditional Japanese clothing, it became popular in the Nara period and remains in use to this day.

Clothes varied in material, with silk and cotton being used by the higher classes. They were usually rather colorful, and traditionally, they covered as much skin as possible. It was regarded that the less skin seen, the higher status of the person wearing the clothes. And these clothes are actually a good metaphor for the ancient Japanese culture in general. It was strict, had certain rules, and it varied between classes. It looks a bit tight and restraining, but it is also very beautiful and full of color and uniqueness. And in every aspect, one can see both indigenous roots and foreign influences. This is what makes Japanese culture, even today, unique, as it is a mix of both old and new, of domestic and native. And those characteristics we can track all the way back to the classical period of Japanese history when the foundations of the Japanese civilization were laid.

Conclusion

Ancient Japan went through various changes through history, from a unified courtly and art-loving country to a militaristic, pragmatic, and divided society. It saw the rise and fall of emperors, nobility, and shōguns in an ever-changing political landscape. Yet it would be wrong to focus solely on the wars and intrigues. Ancient Japanese society left a substantial cultural heritage that became an important part of the world's civilizations. And because of its uniqueness, even today it captivates people's imagination, especially after Japan's economic and cultural renaissance of the late 20th century when its culture became globally recognizable. Looking at it today, we can see traces of old traditions and roots of this great civilization that span almost 2,000 years.

When looking at both Japanese history and its culture, it becomes obvious that it is a civilization of paradoxes and opposites. However, its most striking characteristic, what makes it so unique, is its relations to other civilizations. Be it through pure luck or some higher reasoning, the Japanese throughout the past knew when it was time to open their borders and learn from their surroundings and when it was a good time to close them down and develop their own traditions, building on the influences of others. And they kept doing so even after the ancient times. When the Tokugawa regime solidified its rule, Japan closed its borders in the face of the Western colonizers, saving their country both from exploitation and their culture from being overwhelmed. But in the mid-19th century, when Japan saw that it was falling behind the rest of the world, it reopened its borders. Through the Meiji restoration, it learned from others around the world to create a modern and successful country once again before closing itself from foreign influences in the early 20th century, feeling that the old Japanese traditions were in danger of being forgotten. This ultimately led to the notorious crimes during World War II; however, the Japanese learned from that as well. They realized that the best path is a mixture of sticking to one's own tradition but also leaving a door open for new things to come from outside.

It is exactly that mixture of indigenous traditions, thoughts, and ideas mixed with foreign influences that makes Japanese culture so fascinatingly unique. It is what makes this civilization captivating today, and it is a lesson that every civilization, every nation, every society, and every person today should remember. The road to success is paved with accepting new and mixing it with the old, accepting the unfamiliar and exotic while keeping the local customs alive. This is one of the lessons that history can teach us because it connects the past with the present while keeping an eye on the future. This is why it is important to learn about the past of not only our own cultures and countries but from nations all across the world. Understanding others better will help us better understand ourselves. And that makes us capable of accepting both our own traditions as well as of those that come from different cultures, leading to a healthier world society and a greater future.

Free Bonus from Captivating History (Available for a Limited time)

Hi History Lovers!

Now you have a chance to join our exclusive history list so you can get your first history ebook for free as well as discounts and a potential to get more history books for free! Simply visit the link below to join.

Captivatinghistory.com/ebook

Also, make sure to follow us on Facebook, Twitter and Youtube by searching for Captivating History.

Here's another book by Captivating History that we think you would find interesting

Bibliography

Andressen, Curtis A., *A Short History of Japan: From Samurai to Sony*, Allen & Unwin 2002.

Henshall, Kenneth G., *A History of Japan: From Stone Age to Superpower*, Palgrave Macmillan 2004.

Beasley, W. G., *The Japanese Experience: A Short History of Japan*, Weidenfeld & Nicolson 1999.

Kozo Yamamura, *The Cambridge History of Japan: Vol. 3 Medieval Japan,* Cambridge University Press 1990.

John Whitney Hall, *The Cambridge History of Japan: Vol. 4 Early Modern Japan*, Cambridge University Press 1991.

Delmer M. Brown, *The Cambridge History of Japan: Vol. 1 Ancient Japan*, Cambridge University Press 1993.

Donald Shively and William H. McCullough, *The Cambridge History of Japan: Vol. 2 Heian Japan*, Cambridge University Press 1999.

John A. Ferejohn and Frances McCall Rosenbluth, *War and State Building in Medieval Japan*, Stanford University Press 2010.

Friday, Karl F., *Samurai, Warfare & the State in Early Medieval Japan*, Routledge 2004.

Deal, William E., *Handbook to Life in Medieval and Early Modern Japan*, Facts on File 2006.

Oyler, Elizabeth, *Swords, Oaths, and Prophetic Visions: Authoring Warrior Rule in Medieval Japan*, University of Hawai'i Press 2006.

Stephen Trunbull, *Warriors of Medieval Japan*, Osprey Publishing 2005.

Anthony J. Bryant, *The Samurai*, Osprey Publishing 1989.

CPSIA information can be obtained
at www.ICGtesting.com
Printed in the USA
LVHW052202170221
679358LV00003B/680